2016 Special 301 Report

Acknowledgements

The Office of the United States Trade Representative is responsible for the preparation of this Report. United States Trade Representative Michael Froman gratefully acknowledges the contributions of staff to the writing and production of this Report, and extends his thanks to partner agencies, including the following Departments and agencies: State; Treasury; Justice; Agriculture; Commerce, including the International Trade Administration and the United States Patent and Trademark Office; Labor; Health and Human Services, including the Food and Drug Administration; Homeland Security, including Customs and Border Protection, Immigration and Customs Enforcement, and the National Intellectual Property Rights Coordination Center; and the United States Agency for International Development. Ambassador Froman also recognizes the contributions of the Intellectual Property Enforcement Coordinator as well as those of the United States Copyright Office.

In preparing the Report, substantial information was solicited from U.S. Embassies around the world, from U.S. Government agencies, and from interested stakeholders. The draft of this Report was developed through the Special 301 Subcommittee of the inter-agency Trade Policy Staff Committee.

April 2016

Contents

1
Executive Summary

7
Section I: Developments in Intellectual Property Rights Protection, Enforcement, and Related Market Access

29
Section II: Country Reports

29
Priority Watch List

50
Watch List

65
Annex 1: Special 301 Statutory Basis

67
Annex 2: United States Government-Sponsored Technical Assistance and Capacity Building

Executive Summary

The Special 301 Report (Report) is the result of an annual review of the state of intellectual property rights (IPR) protection and enforcement in U.S. trading partners around the world, which the Office of the United States Trade Representative (USTR) conducts pursuant to Section 182 of the Trade Act of 1974, as amended by the Omnibus Trade and Competitiveness Act of 1988, the Uruguay Round Agreements Act, and the Trade Facilitation and Trade Enforcement Act of 2015 (19 U.S.C. § 2242).

This Report reflects the Administration's continued resolve to encourage and maintain adequate and effective IPR protection and enforcement worldwide. The Report identifies a wide range of concerns, including: (a) the deterioration in IPR protection and enforcement in a number of trading partners; (b) reported inadequacies in trade secret protection in China, India, and elsewhere; (c) troubling "indigenous innovation" policies that may unfairly disadvantage U.S. right holders in markets abroad; (d) the continuing challenges of online copyright piracy; (e) measures that impede market access for U.S. products embodying IPR and U.S. entities that rely upon IPR protection; and (f) other ongoing, systemic IPR enforcement issues in many trading partners around the world.

The Report serves a critical function by identifying opportunities and challenges facing U.S. innovative and creative industries in foreign markets and by promoting job creation, economic development, and many other benefits that effective IPR protection and enforcement support. The Report informs the public and our trading partners and seeks to be a positive catalyst for change. USTR looks forward to working closely with the governments of the trading partners that are identified in this year's Report to address both emerging and continuing concerns, and to build on the positive results that many of these governments have achieved.

The Special 301 Process

The Congressionally mandated annual Special 301 Report is the result of an extensive multi stakeholder process. Pursuant to the statute mandating the Report, USTR is charged with designating as Priority Foreign Countries those countries that have the most onerous or egregious acts, policies, or practices and whose acts, policies, or practices have the greatest adverse impact (actual or potential) on the relevant U.S. products. (See **ANNEX 1**). To facilitate administration of the statute, USTR has created a Priority Watch List and Watch List within this Report. Placement of a trading partner on the Priority Watch List or Watch List indicates that particular problems exist in that country with respect to IPR protection, enforcement, or market access for persons relying on IPR.

On February 24, 2016, President Obama signed the bipartisan Trade Facilitation and Trade

Enforcement Act of 2015 into law. Provisions of this new law amend the Special 301 statute to direct USTR to develop action plans for each country that USTR identifies as a Priority Watch List country and that has been on the Priority Watch List for at least one year. The new law also specifically instructs USTR to consider whether foreign countries provide adequate and effective means for U.S. persons to secure, exercise and enforce their rights relating to trade secrets. With this legislation, Congress and the President have reaffirmed the importance of strong IPR protection and enforcement for the U.S. economy and have strengthened the Administration's tools for holding trading partners accountable for intellectual property related trade practices that disadvantage America's creators and innovators.

Public Engagement

USTR solicited broad public participation in the 2016 Special 301 review process to facilitate sound, well balanced assessments of trading partners' IPR protection and enforcement and related market access issues affecting IPR intensive industries, and to help ensure that the Special 301 review would be based on comprehensive information regarding IPR issues in trading partner markets.

USTR requested written submissions from the public through a notice published in the *Federal Register* on January 11, 2016 (**Federal Register notice**). In addition, on March 2, 2016, USTR conducted a public hearing that provided the opportunity for interested persons to testify before the inter agency Special 301 Subcommittee of the Trade Policy Staff Committee (TPSC) about issues relevant to the review. The hearing featured testimony from witnesses, including representatives of foreign governments, industry, academics, and non governmental organizations. USTR recorded and posted on its public website the testimony received at the Special 301 hearing, and offered a post hearing comment period during which hearing participants and interested parties could submit additional information in support of, or in response to, hearing testimony. The *Federal Register* notice and post hearing comment opportunity drew submissions from 62 interested parties, including 16 trading partner governments.

The submissions filed in response to the *Federal Register* notice, and during the post hearing comment period, are available to the public online at WWW.REGULATIONS.GOV, docket number USTR 2015 0022. The public can access both the **video** and **transcript** of the hearing at www.USTR.GOV.

Country Placement

The Special 301 listings and actions announced in this Report are the result of intensive deliberations among all relevant agencies within the U.S. Government, informed by extensive consultations with participating stakeholders, foreign governments, the U.S. Congress, and other interested parties.

USTR, together with the Special 301 Subcommittee, conducts a broad and balanced assessment of U.S. trading partners' IPR protection and enforcement, as well as related market access issues affecting IPR intensive industries, in accordance with the statutory criteria. (*See* **ANNEX 1**). The Special 301 Subcommittee, through the TPSC, provides country placement recommendations to the USTR based on this assessment.

This assessment is necessarily conducted on a case by case basis, taking into account diverse factors such as a trading partner's level of development, its international obligations and commitments, the concerns of right holders and other interested parties, and the trade and investment policies of the United States. It is informed by the various cross cutting issues and trends identified in **Section I**. Each assessment is based upon the specific facts and circumstances that shape IPR protection and enforcement in a particular trading partner.

In the year ahead, USTR will continue to engage trading partners that are discussed in this Report. In preparation for, and in the course of, those interactions, USTR will:

- Engage with U.S. stakeholders, the U.S. Congress, and other interested parties to ensure that the U.S. Government's position is informed by the full range of views on the pertinent issues;

- Conduct extensive discussions with individual trading partners regarding their respective IPR regimes;

- Encourage trading partners to engage fully, and with the greatest degree of transparency, with the full range of stakeholders on IPR matters;

- Develop action plans with benchmarks for each country that has been on the Priority Watch List for at least one year to encourage progress on high priority IP concerns; and

- Identify, where possible, appropriate ways in which the U.S. Government can be of assistance. (See **ANNEX 2**).

USTR will conduct these discussions in a manner that both advances the policy goals of the United States and respects the importance of meaningful policy dialogue with U.S. trading partners. In addition, USTR will continue to work closely with other U.S. Government agencies to ensure consistency of U.S. trade policy objectives with other Administration policies.

The 2016 Special 301 List

The Special 301 Subcommittee reviewed 73 trading partners during the 2016 Special 301 process. The Subcommittee received stakeholder input on more than 100 trading partners, but focused its review on those submissions that responded to the request set forth in the notice published in the *Federal Register* to identify whether a particular trading partner should be named as a Priority Foreign Country (PFC), placed on the Priority Watch List (PWL) or Watch List (WL), or not listed in the Report. Following extensive research and analysis, USTR has listed 34 trading partners as follows:

Priority Watch List	Watch List	
- Algeria	- Barbados	- Jamaica
- Argentina	- Bolivia	- Lebanon
- Chile	- Brazil	- Mexico
- China	- Bulgaria	- Pakistan
- India	- Canada	- Peru
- Indonesia	- Colombia	- Romania
- Kuwait	- Costa Rica	- Switzerland
- Russia	- Dominican Republic	- Turkey
- Thailand	- Ecuador	- Turkmenistan
- Ukraine	- Egypt	- Uzbekistan
- Venezuela	- Greece	- Vietnam
	- Guatemala	

Out-of-Cycle Reviews

An Out of Cycle Review (OCR) is a tool that USTR uses to encourage progress on IPR issues of concern. OCRs provide an opportunity to address and remedy such issues through heightened engagement and cooperation with trading partners and other stakeholders.

Country-Specific Out-of-Cycle Reviews

OCRs focus on identified IPR challenges in specific trading partner markets. Successful resolution of specific IPR issues of concern can lead to a positive change in a trading partner's Special 301 status outside of the typical time frame for the annual review. Conversely, failure to address identified IPR concerns, or further deterioration as to an IPR related concern within the specified timeframe, can lead to an adverse change in status.

In the coming months, USTR will conduct four OCRs with the following trading partners:

- USTR will conduct an OCR of **Colombia**, which is currently on the Watch List, to assess Colombia's commitment to the IP provisions of the United States Colombia Trade Promotion Agreement and to monitor the implementation of Colombia's National Development Plan. Given relevant upcoming opportunities for review and other relevant factors, USTR will determine at four month intervals (i.e., in August and December) whether to adjust or maintain Colombia's Special 301 status.

- USTR will conduct an OCR of **Pakistan** in the fall of 2016 to determine whether Pakistan fulfills commitments it made during the 2016 annual review cycle to continue to improve certain aspects of IPR protection and enforcement in Pakistan.

- Although **Spain** is not listed in the 2016 Report, USTR continues the OCR of Spain, announced in 2013, which is focused, in particular, on concrete steps taken by Spain to combat copyright piracy over the Internet. USTR welcomes the significant and positive actions Spain has taken over the past year, including with respect to the passage of amendments to legislation and to the issuance of a revised Attorney General's circular, and urges Spain to continue its work in this area, such as regarding the Intellectual Property Commission to ensure the adequacy of its resources, the implementation of its new legal authorities, and the effectiveness of its operations and actions.

- **Tajikistan** is removed from the Watch List in 2016 in recognition of Tajikistan's efforts to improve IPR protection and enforcement, including providing *ex officio* authority to customs authorities; acceding to international IPR treaties that contain obligations to strengthen IPR protection and enforcement (e.g., the Singapore Treaty on the Law of Trademarks, the Hague Agreement Concerning the International Registration of Industrial Designs, the Protocol Relating to the Madrid Agreement Concerning the International Registration of Marks (Madrid Protocol), WIPO Copyright Treaty (WCT) and WIPO Performances and Phonograms Treaty (WPPT)); and adopting amendments to provide a system for protecting against the unfair commercial use, as well as unauthorized disclosure, of undisclosed test or other data generated to obtain marketing approval for pharmaceutical and agricultural chemical products. The OCR of Tajikistan announced in 2015 will remain open through the fall of 2016 to reinforce the positive steps Tajikistan has taken to strengthen IPR. In 2016, USTR encourages Tajikistan to focus efforts to complete the benchmark set out in the OCR by formalizing a presidential level decree, law, or regulation mandating government use of licensed software by the fall of 2016. Tajikistan has established a working group, headed by the First Deputy Minister of

Economic Development and Trade, to oversee this process. If Tajikistan is unable to meet the fall 2016 deadline, USTR may reconsider Tajikistan's Special 301 status.

USTR may conduct additional OCRs of other trading partners as circumstances warrant, or as requested by the trading partner.

Out-of-Cycle Review of Notorious Markets

In 2010, USTR began publishing annually the *Notorious Markets List* as an OCR separately from the annual Special 301 Report. The *Notorious Markets List* identifies selected online and physical markets that are reportedly engaged in copyright piracy and trademark counterfeiting, according to information submitted to USTR in response to a notice published in the *Federal Register* requesting public comments. In 2015, USTR requested such comments on September 10 and published the 2015 Notorious Markets List on December 22. USTR plans to conduct its next OCR of Notorious Markets in the fall of 2016.

Structure of the Special 301 Report

The 2016 Report contains the following Sections and Annexes:

SECTION I: DEVELOPMENTS IN INTELLECTUAL PROPERTY RIGHTS PROTECTION AND ENFORCEMENT AND RELATED MARKET ACCESS discusses global trends and issues in IPR protection and enforcement and related market access that the U.S. Government works to address on a daily basis;

SECTION II: COUNTRY REPORTS includes descriptions of issues of concern with respect to particular trading partners;

ANNEX 1: SPECIAL 301 STATUTORY BASIS describes the statutory basis of the Special 301 Report; and

ANNEX 2: UNITED STATES GOVERNMENT-SPONSORED TECHNICAL ASSISTANCE AND CAPACITY BUILDING highlights U.S. Government sponsored technical assistance and capacity building efforts.

SECTION I
Developments in Intellectual Property Rights Protection, Enforcement, and Related Market Access

An important mission of USTR and other U.S. Government agencies is to support and implement the Administration's commitment to protect vigorously the interests of American holders of IPR in other countries while preserving the incentives that ensure access to, and widespread dissemination of, the fruits of innovation and creativity. IPR infringement, including trademark counterfeiting and copyright piracy[1], causes significant financial losses for right holders and legitimate businesses around the world. It undermines U.S. comparative advantages in innovation and creativity, to the detriment of American businesses and workers. In its most pernicious forms, IPR infringement endangers the public. Some counterfeit products, including semiconductors, automobile parts, and medicines, pose significant risks to consumer health and safety. In addition, trade in counterfeit and pirated products often fuels cross-border organized criminal networks and hinders sustainable economic development in many countries.

Because fostering innovation and creativity is essential to U.S. prosperity, competitiveness, and the support of an estimated 40 million U.S. jobs that directly or indirectly rely on IPR-intensive industries, USTR works to protect American innovation and creativity with all the tools of U.S. trade policy, including through this Report.

Initiatives to Strengthen IPR Protection and Enforcement Internationally

Positive Developments

The United States welcomes the following important developments in 2015 and early 2016:

- In 2015, **China** continued to pursue a broad ranging overhaul of its intellectual property related laws and regulations, as well as a pilot study of specialized intellectual property courts. At least some portions of the draft revised laws and regulations appear to be consistent with recommendations offered by the United States and statements by the Government of China expressing a commitment to protect and enforce IPR; to allow industry and entrepreneurs a greater voice in policy development; and to allow market mechanisms to play a greater role in

[1] The terms "trademark counterfeiting" and "copyright piracy" may appear below also as "counterfeiting" and "piracy," respectively.

guiding research and development (R&D) efforts. The United States urges China to continue to engage with foreign governments and stakeholders and to ensure that legal and regulatory reforms adhere to these articulated commitments.

- In June 2015, the U.S. National Intellectual Property Rights Coordination Center (IPR Center) and the General Administration of Customs **China** (GACC) signed an IPR addendum that expanded on a MOU the countries drafted in 2011 to collaborate on the enforcement of customs laws. This IPR addendum will help both China and the United States combat IPR infringement by tracking IPR violations, sharing information, and monitoring the illicit importation, exportation, or trafficking of counterfeit trademarked merchandise. The United States and China will also conduct joint training operations targeting counterfeit products sent between the two countries that pose a health and safety risk. Further, in December 2015, U.S. Customs and Border Protection (CBP), U.S. Immigration and Customs Enforcement/Homeland Security Investigations (ICE/HSI), and the GACC participated in a bilateral working group meeting and agreed to an ambitious agenda of "customs authority to customs authority" cooperation for the upcoming year.

- The Government of **Honduras**, which was not listed in the 2015 Special Report, has taken significant actions to improve IPR protection and enforcement in that country. Pursuant to an OCR announced in the 2015 Report, the Government of Honduras committed to a detailed Intellectual Property Work Plan for 2016 focusing on, among other things, strengthening criminal IPR enforcement, combating the unauthorized rebroadcast of cable and satellite transmissions, clarifying the scope of protections for geographical indications (GIs), and developing a trademark recordation system to improve customs border enforcement. Honduras has taken actions to implement the plan, including by increasing the number of dedicated criminal IP prosecutors and publishing certain generic terms ineligible for protection as GIs. Based on these welcome commitments and actions to date, the OCR is concluded with no change in status, although continued review of and adherence to the Work Plan is critical. The United States applauds Honduras's commitments as reflected in the Work Plan and its actions to date and expects that Honduras's approach will serve as a model for similarly situated countries in Central America. In this regard, the United States welcomes **Costa Rica**'s recent commitment to develop and implement an IP Work Plan, in consultation with the United States.

- **Paraguay** was removed from the Special 301 Watch List in 2015 pursuant to an OCR. The United States and Paraguay signed a Memorandum of Understanding (MOU) on Intellectual Property Rights in June 2015, under which Paraguay committed to take specific steps to improve its IPR protection and enforcement environment. Additionally, the MOU solidifies bilateral cooperation through which the United States supports Paraguay's efforts to strengthen IPR protection and enforcement. The United States will monitor Paraguay's progress under the MOU and looks forward to continued cooperation with Paraguay in 2016.

- Several countries joined the global trend toward extending the term of protection for copyright, creating greater market opportunities overseas for U.S. and domestic right holders. **Canada** extended the term of protection for sound recordings to 70 years, and **Jamaica** also passed legislation to extend the term of copyright protection.

- Administrative and judicial copyright enforcement continues to improve in **Italy**. A November 2015 court case confirmed that the primary purpose of circumvention devices was to play pirated video games and that security measures are protected under Italian law. The antipiracy framework under the Italian Communications Regulatory Authority (AGCOM) had enforcement successes against off shore infringing torrent sites thanks to fast track procedures and tools designed to address illegal linking sites and repeat infringers. Furthermore, the Italian Constitutional Court upheld the legitimacy of the AGCOM regulatory framework.

- **Belarus** is removed from the Watch List this year. Over the past several years Belarus has shown continued commitment to improve its laws on IPR protection and enforcement, including an ongoing upgrade of the National Center for Intellectual Property's automated systems. In 2015, Belarus amended its administrative and criminal codes to strengthen penalties for repeat infringers. Also in 2015, authorities in Belarus worked with enforcement authorities in other countries on joint IPR enforcement initiatives. Authorities, including the Ministry of Interior, have launched investigations and seized counterfeit and pirated products, and courts have issued convictions under the criminal code with respect to IP related crimes.

- Over the past year, the Government of **Kenya** has taken significant steps to improve the protection and enforcement of IPR. In 2015, Kenya allocated more resources to the Anti Counterfeit Agency, including opening two new branch offices and hiring additional enforcement officers. The Kenyan government has also drafted updates to their copyright and trademark legislation, which if adopted, will strengthen IPR protection and enforcement, such as by creating legal incentives for Internet service providers (ISPs) to cooperate with copyright holders and creating deterrent penalties for infringement. The United States welcomes these positive developments in Kenya. Furthermore, the United States encourages other sub Saharan African countries, such as **Nigeria**, that are entry points into Africa for counterfeit and pirated goods often threatening health and safety similarly to address the factors that undermine effective IPR protection and enforcement. By working individually and collectively with other countries in the region, as well as with source nations such as China, countries in sub Saharan Africa can bring a renewed focus to this challenge.

- As of April 2016, 55 countries have become members of the 1991 Act of the International Union for the Protection of New Varieties of Plants Convention (**UPOV 91**). **Canada**, **Montenegro**, and **Tanzania** are the latest to join UPOV 91. The UPOV Convention requires member countries to grant IPR protection to breeders of new plant varieties, known as the breeder's rights. An effective plant variety protection (PVP) system incentivizes plant breeding activities, which leads to increased numbers of new plant varieties with improved characteristics such as high yield, tolerance to adverse environmental conditions, and better food quality. In addition, promoting strong plant variety protection and enforcement globally helps improve industry competitiveness in foreign markets, provides access to foreign plant varieties, and enhances domestic breeding programs. Joining, ratifying, and implementing UPOV 91 is an important feature of recent trade agreements, including the recently concluded Trans Pacific Partnership Agreement (TPP).

- As of April 2016, there are 94 Parties to the World Intellectual Property Organization (WIPO) Performances and Phonograms Treaty (WPPT) and 94 Parties to the WIPO Copyright Treaty (WCT), collectively known as the **WIPO Internet Treaties**. These treaties, completed in 1996 and which entered into force in 2002, have raised the standard of copyright protection around the world, particularly with regard to Internet based delivery of copyrighted content. The treaties, which include certain exclusive rights, require signatories to provide adequate legal protection and effective legal remedies against the circumvention of technological protection measures (TPMs) as well as certain acts affecting rights management information. **Burundi** became a party to the WCT on April 12, 2016. During the past year, other trading partners, such as **Jamaica**, have implemented key provisions of the WIPO Internet Treaties in their national laws to create a legal environment conducive to investment and growth in legitimate Internet related businesses, services, and technologies.

The United States will continue to work with its trading partners to further enhance IPR protection and enforcement during the coming year.

Best IPR Practices by Trading Partners

USTR highlights the following best practices by trading partners in the area of IPR protection and enforcement:

- USTR supports **predictability, transparency, and meaningful engagement between governments and stakeholders** in the development of national laws, regulations, procedures, and other measures. Stakeholders report that such transparency and participation allow governments to avoid unintended consequences and facilitate stakeholder compliance with legislative and regulatory changes. For example, in late 2015, **India** issued a draft for public comment of proposed amendments to India's Patents Rules and held hearings with interested stakeholders. USTR encourages continued, meaningful engagement with interested stakeholders as India continues to develop these and other IPR related laws and regulations. The United States urges trading partners, such as **Thailand**, to take steps to improve in this area.

- **Cooperation and coordination among government agencies** is another example of a best practice. Several countries, including the United States, have introduced IPR enforcement coordination mechanisms or agreements to enhance inter agency cooperation. In this year's review, stakeholders reported positively on the efforts of DINAPI the National Directorate for Intellectual Property in **Paraguay** to increase interagency cooperation. Similarly, an interagency Special Anti Piracy Task Force in **Malaysia** has made progress in deterring and preventing infringing distribution networks. The United States encourages other trading partners to consider adopting similar cooperative IPR arrangements.

- **Specialized IP enforcement units** that focus on and understand IPR enforcement have proven to be important catalysts in the fight against counterfeiting and piracy. The specialized IP police unit in Rio de Janeiro, **Brazil** could be a model for other cities in the country and around the world. Another example includes the Special Internet Forensics Unit in **Malaysia's** Ministry of Domestic Trade, Cooperatives, and Consumerism responsible for IPR enforcement. While only recently created, USTR hopes to be able to highlight the IP Digital Crime Unit of **Mexico** as a best practice in the future.

- Several trading partners have participated, or supported participation, in **innovative mechanisms that enable government and private sector right holders to donate or license pharmaceutical patents voluntarily and on mutually-agreed terms and conditions**. In these arrangements, parties use existing patent rights to facilitate the diffusion of technology in support of public policy goals. The United States was the first government to share patents with the Medicines Patent Pool, an independent foundation hosted by the World Health Organization (WHO). The United States encourages additional public and private patent holders to explore voluntary licenses with the Medicines Patent Pool as one of many innovative ways to help improve the availability of medicines in developing countries. The patents that the United States shared were related to protease inhibitor medicines, primarily used to treat drug resistant HIV infections. In addition, the United States, **Brazil**, and **South Africa** par ticipate as providers in the WIPO Re:Search Consortium, a voluntary mechanism for making IPR and know how available on mutually agreed terms and conditions to the global health research community to find cures or treatments for Neglected Tropical Diseases, malaria, and tuberculosis. Other countries participate as supporters. These arrangements have been used successfully to enhance access to medicines.

- A best practice in **raising awareness on IPR protection** is the creation of public private partnerships. In Lebanon, the Beirut based Brand Protection Group (BPG) collaborates closely with the Government of Lebanon to provide workshops at local universities, roundtables with relevant government ministries, and capacity building programs for local officials. **The Philippines** develops informational material in partnership with international organizations such as the Business Action to Stop Counterfeiting and Piracy (BASCAP).

- The **use and procurement of licensed software by government agencies** sets the right example for private enterprises. Government agencies in **Mexico**, including the Ministry of Economy, the Tax Administration (SAT) and the Mexico Institute of Industrial Property (IMPI) have all obtained Verafirm Certification which confirms that the agencies' software asset management procedures (SAM) are aligned with the SAM standard of the International Standards Organization.

- Another best practice is the active participation of government officials in **technical assistance and capacity building**. As further explained in Annex 2, the United States encourages foreign governments to make training opportunities available to their officials and actively engages with trading partners in capacity building efforts both in the United States and abroad.

Multilateral and Plurilateral Initiatives

The United States works to promote adequate and effective IPR protection and enforcement through the following mechanisms:

- **Trans-Pacific Partnership**: In February 2016, the United States, along with Australia, Brunei Darussalam, Canada, Chile, Japan, Malaysia, Mexico, New Zealand, Peru, Singapore, and Vietnam, signed the TPP Agreement.

Drawing from and building on other bilateral and regional trade agreements, the TPP Agreement includes commitments to protect IP and to combat counterfeiting, piracy, and other infringement, including trade secret theft; obligations to facilitate legitimate digital trade, including trade in creative content; and provisions to promote development of, and access to, innovative and generic medicines. Complete fact sheets summarizing the many ways in which the TPP is Promoting Innovation and Creativity and Promoting Digital Trade are available on HTTPS://USTR.GOV/TPP/ as well as full summaries and text of all the commitments in the IP Chapter. The TPP Agreement's Intellectual Property Chapter addresses many of the challenges to adequate and effective IPR protection and enforcement outlined in this Report, including:

Copyright: The TPP IP Chapter encourages practices that are fair, efficient, transparent and accountable regarding the collection and distribution of copyright royalties. The TPP requires countries to provide for works a minimum term of copyright protection of author's life plus 70 years, and for works that have terms calculated based on publication date, like movies and recordings, a term of copyright protection of 70 years. The TPP will also require Parties to establish systems to help address Internet copyright infringement in an effective manner through copyright safe harbors for legitimate ISPs. In addition, the TPP includes provisions prohibiting the circumvention of, and the trafficking in devices that circumvent, TPMs.

Trademarks and Geographical Indications: The TPP IP Chapter Agreement promotes efficient and transparent registration of trademarks, including through electronic trademark registration systems, streamlined procedures aimed at reducing red tape, and increased regional harmonization of trademark systems. The TPP also requires Parties to provide protection for certification and collective trademarks.

The TPP IP Chapter also contains a variety of transparency and due process safeguards that relate to domestic legal regimes regarding GIs. These safeguards aim to protect the interests of producers and traders that have pre existing trademark rights or that rely on the use of common product names against market access barriers and other negative impacts caused by legal regimes that provide overly broad protection of GIs. (*See* **Geographical Indications**). For example, the TPP requires Parties to provide opportunities to oppose the grant or recognition of new GIs, as well as opportunities to seek cancellation of previously granted or recognized GIs and specifies particular grounds that must be available in these proceedings. The TPP sets forth guidelines for determining generic (or commonly used) terms in each market. The TPP also extends many of these obligations to translations or transliterations of GIs. Collectively, these TPP provisions aim to help close loopholes that have hurt U.S. producers and traders.

Trade Secrets: The TPP IP Chapter requires Parties to provide the legal means to prevent the misappropriation of trade secrets and corporate espionage. The TPP is the first U.S. trade agreement to require criminal penalties for trade secret theft, including cyber theft. This is a significant step forward for TPP Parties, and an important precedent in a region where U.S. companies have faced significant challenges as a result of such activity. (*See* **Trade Secrets**). The TPP trade secrets provision does not prevent legitimate disclosures, such as disclosures by whistleblowers.

Patents: A strong, transparent and fair patent system is essential to protecting inventions and incentivizing new innovation. The TPP includes the obligation to make patents available for any invention including products and processes, in any field of technology if the invention is new, involves an inventive step, and is capable of industrial application. In addition, the TPP recognizes the importance of incremental innovation through an additional obligation that requires Parties to make patents available for a new use of a known product, a new method of using a known product, or a new process of using a known product. This will help ensure that patent applications for inventions that are otherwise novel, non obvious, and useful are not rejected merely because they are related to a known product. The TPP also confirms that patents are available for inventions derived from plants, another active area of innovation. Inventors will also benefit from a 12 month patent grace period to allow certain public disclosures without disqualifying an invention from meeting patentability requirements for novelty or non obviousness. The TPP also provides for patent term adjustment for unreasonable patent office delays in the issuance of patents for inventions, including pharmaceuticals, such as those caused by the backlogs present in many countries on the Watch List and Priority Watch List.

Pharmaceuticals: The TPP sets a minimum standard of at least five years of data protection for new pharmaceutical products and, for the first time in any trade agreement, the TPP requires an extended period of effective market protection for new biologics. The TPP clarifies that the period of protection will start on the date of approval in each market, rather than from the first marketing approval in the world. In addition, the TPP requires Parties to provide for advance notice, adequate time and opportunity, and procedures for patent holders to seek timely resolution of patent disputes prior to the marketing of an alleged infringing product. The TPP also obligates Parties to provide an extension of the patent term when the marketing approval process unreasonably cuts into the effective term of a patent of a pharmaceutical product.

Enforcement: TPP Parties are obligated to provide mechanisms – including civil and administrative procedures and remedies, provisional measures, border measures, and criminal enforcement – to address many of the challenges of counterfeiting and piracy described in this Report, including digital IP theft and supply chains for the manufacture and distribution of counterfeit goods. (See **Digital Piracy, Piracy Online, and Broadcast Piracy** and **Border and Criminal Enforcement Against Counterfeiting**). The TPP requires Parties to adopt measures to address cable and satellite signal piracy and the unauthorized camcording of movies in theaters. Enforcement provisions are also designed to close loopholes exploited by counterfeiters in many countries and to target counterfeit products that pose threats to consumer health and safety. The TPP also ensures that border officials and enforcement authorities may act on their own initiative (*ex officio*) to identify and seize imported and exported counterfeit and pirated goods. Additionally, the TPP is the first trade agreement to clarify that Parties must subject state-owned enterprises (SOEs) to IP enforcement rules, subject to certain disciplines in the Agreement on Trade-Related Aspects of Intellectual Property Rights (TRIPS).

- **Transatlantic Trade and Investment Partnership (T-TIP):** The United States and the EU provide among the highest levels of IPR protection and enforcement in the world. In the T-TIP, the United States is pursuing a targeted approach on IPR that will reflect the shared United States-EU objective of high-level IPR protection and enforcement, and sustained and enhanced joint leadership on IPR issues. The United States will seek new opportunities to advance and defend the interests of U.S. creators, innovators, businesses, farmers, ranchers, and workers with respect to strong protection and effective enforcement of IPR, including the ability to compete in foreign markets. The United States and the EU have held thirteen rounds of negotiations, most recently in April 2016.

- **World Trade Organization (WTO):** The multilateral structure of the WTO provides opportunities for USTR to lead engagement with trading partners on IPR issues, including through trade policy reviews, accession negotiations for prospective Members, the Council for Trade-Related Aspects of Intellectual Property Rights (TRIPS Council), and the Dispute Settlement Body. In the past year, the United States sponsored discussions in the TRIPS Council on the positive and mutually reinforcing relationship between innovation and the protection and enforcement of IPR.

In March 2016, for example, the United States, Australia, the EU, Hong Kong, Japan, Peru, Russia, Singapore, and Taiwan sponsored an initiative in the TRIPS Council entitled, "IP and Innovation: Education and Diffusion." Joined by WTO members from five continents, including developed, developing, and least developed countries, the United States detailed how education is an innovation and creativity accelerator in terms of generating ideas as well as diffusing innovation and creativity. In its intervention, the United States enumerated numerous education initiatives particularly with respect to science, technology, engineering, and math (STEM) that advance U.S. innovation objectives, including federal government, public private, and stakeholder programs involving IPR education. Many interventions echoed the importance of incorporating IPR into education curricula as an essential part of any innovation strategy to ensure that our innovators understand not only how to protect their hard work, but how to use IPR to grow resources for future R&D, attract investment, structure collaboration and partnerships, create jobs, and adapt existing innovations, among other critical objectives.

In October 2015, the United States advanced an agenda on the integral linkage between innovation, entrepreneurship, and economic growth, including exchanges of information between a broad and diverse set of developed and developing countries on economic data, commercial experience, and government policymaking in this area. IPR, innovation, and entrepreneurship are intrinsically linked. Innovators are frequently our entrepreneurs, who in turn rely heavily on IPR to attract investment, protect their new technologies from theft, and generate revenue for future research, development, commercialization, and employment. And together, IPR, innovation, and entrepreneurship play a critical developmental role. The case studies that delegations explored at the Council confirm vividly what the theoretical and empirical literature amply demonstrates. IPR play a critical role in delivering on the promise of the world's entrepreneurs, whose innovative new technologies fuel domestic and international economic growth, and help raise global standards of living.

In June 2015, the United States led an initiative in the TRIPS Council to emphasize the vital role IPR plays in attracting capital and investment to fuel innovation. The initiative underscored the important linkage between IPR and financing for capital intensive R&D, and demonstrated how increased respect for IPR can not only increase access to, but also lower the cost of, investment for innovative businesses and startups. Representatives from the United States shared stories on the critical role of investors, like banks, stock markets, venture capital, and angel investors, in the innovation life cycle, from early R&D to later stage manufacturing and commercialization. These stories shed light on how IP protection can reduce the financial risk associated with innovation, and enhance the economic and social benefits achieved with R&D investment.

Bilateral and Regional Initiatives

The United States works with many trading partners to strengthen IPR protection and enforcement through the provisions of bilateral agreements, including trade agreements and bilateral memoranda of cooperation, and through regional initiatives.

The following are examples of bilateral coordination and cooperation:

- The **United States-China Joint Commission on Commerce and Trade (JCCT)** and the **United States-China Strategic and Economic Dialogue (S&ED)** are two very significant bilateral annual trade engagements through which the United States negotiates important IP and innovation commitments with China.

- **Trade and Investment Framework Agreements (TIFAs)** between the United States and more than 50 trading partners and regions around the world have facilitated discussions on enhancing IPR protection and enforcement. For example, at the ninth United States Taiwan TIFA Council meeting in Taipei in October 2015, the United States welcomed **Taiwan's** announcement of steps to improve the protection and enforcement of IPR, including by increasing human and financial resources for Taiwan's IPR enforcement authorities, addressing piracy occurring in and around university campuses, and taking steps to foster innovation in the pharmaceutical sector. The United States will continue to work with Taiwan under the TIFA to implement the commitments in these areas and engage Taiwan authorities as they amend Taiwan's Copyright Act.

In 2015 2016, the United States signed bilateral TIFAs with **Argentina**, **Armenia**, and **Laos**, creating a forum with each country for bilateral engagement on IPR protection among other trade related issues.

The following are examples of regional coordination and cooperation:

- In the **Asia-Pacific Economic Cooperation (APEC) Intellectual Property Experts Group (IPEG)**, the United States continues to lead an initiative toward the identification of best practices in trade secret protection in APEC economies, as well as other efforts to enhance protection and enforcement of trade secrets. In November 2015, APEC ministers welcomed this work; noted that trade secrets are useful in helping micro , small , and medium sized enterprises to integrate globally; and directed economies to complete work on best practices at the earliest possible time.

- Under its practice of conducting **trade preference program reviews**, USTR, in coordination with other U.S. Government agencies, reviews IPR practices in connection with the implementation of Congressionally authorized trade preference programs, such as the Generalized System of Preferences program, and regional programs, including the African Growth and Opportunity Act, Caribbean Basin Economic Recovery Act, and Caribbean Basin Trade Partnership Act, and works with trading partners to address any policies and practices that may adversely affect their eligibility.

- In 2015, the United States continued to engage with members of the **Caribbean Community and Common Market (CARICOM)** and other governments in the region on concerns regarding inadequate and ineffective copyright protection and enforcement. Heightened engagement on this regional basis, led by the regional IP attaché, resulted in measurable improvements. In **Trinidad & Tobago**, the Telecommunications Authority of Trinidad & Tobago (TATT) took concrete steps to enforce its concessions agreement that requires broadcasters to respect IPR and to obtain all required permissions from IP owners prior to broadcasting programs, information, and other material. TATT set a December 31, 2015 deadline for operators to come into compliance spurring operators to remove several unauthorized channels. TATT is conducting an audit and has pledged to take further enforcement action. In recognition of this commitment to copyright enforcement and on the basis that enforcement actions will continue, Trinidad & Tobago is removed from the Watch List this year. **Jamaica's** Broadcasting Commission has also taken positive steps described further in **Section II**. The United States commends government authorities in Trinidad and Tobago and Jamaica and encourages the region to look to these actions as good examples of first steps governments can take to address a complex and challenging problem.

The United States remains seriously concerned by reports that U.S. songwriters, composers, and music publishers are reportedly not compensated or undercompensated for the public performance of their musical works on TV and radio broadcasts and via cable transmissions in **Antigua & Barbuda, Bahamas, Barbados, Belize, Dominica, Grenada, Guyana, Jamaica, St.**

Lucia, St. Vincent & the Grenadines**, and **Trinidad & Tobago**. Broadcast piracy of free to air and premium services continue throughout the region, undermining investments in creating and distributing content for Belize, Cayman Islands, Guyana, Jamaica, Sint Maarten, Suriname, and Turks & Caicos. The United States urges copyright and broadcast authorities to address the increase in Internet piracy, as well as the use of unauthorized decoding equipment and unlicensed streaming services through amendments to laws and regulations and technical training where needed. The United States looks forward to continuing to engage on these challenges with CARICOM and its member governments. (See Section II and the 2015 and 2014 Special 301 Reports for a more detailed discussion).

In addition to the work described above, the United States anticipates engaging with its trading partners on IPR related initiatives in multilateral and regional fora such as the G 7, WIPO, the Organization for Economic Cooperation and Development (OECD), and the World Customs Organization (WCO). Another example, is the Anti Counterfeiting Trade Agreement (ACTA) effort, launched in October 2007, which brought together a number of countries prepared to embrace strengthened IPR enforcement and cooperative enforcement practices. ACTA signatories are Australia, Canada, Japan, Mexico, Morocco, New Zealand, Singapore, South Korea, and the United States. USTR, in coordination with other U.S. Government agencies, looks forward to continuing engagement with trading partners in bilateral, regional, plurilateral, and multilateral fora to improve the global IPR environment.

IPR Protection and Enforcement and Related Market Access Challenges

Border and Criminal Enforcement Against Counterfeiting

The problem of trademark counterfeiting continues on a global scale and involves the production and sale of a vast array of fake goods. Counterfeited goods, including semiconductors and other electronics, chemicals, automotive and aircraft parts, medicines, food and beverages, household consumer products, personal care products, apparel and footwear, toys, and sporting goods, make their way from **China** and other source countries directly to purchasers around the world and indirectly through transit hubs, including **Indonesia** and the **United Arab Emirates**, to third country markets such as **Brazil**, **Nigeria**, and **Thailand** that are reported to have ineffective or inadequate IPR enforcement systems.

Trademark counterfeiting harms consumers, legitimate producers, and governments. Consumers may be harmed by fraudulent and potentially dangerous counterfeit products, particularly medicines, automotive and airplane parts, and food and beverages that may not be subjected to the rigorous "good manufacturing practices" used for legitimate products. Producers and their employees face diminished revenue and investment incentives, an adverse employment impact, and loss of reputation when consumers purchase fake products. Governments may lose tax revenue and find it more difficult to attract investment because infringers generally do not pay taxes or appropriate duties and often disregard product quality and performance.

In particular, the manufacture and distribution of pharmaceutical products and active pharmaceutical ingredients bearing counterfeit trademarks is a growing problem that has important consequences for consumer health and safety. Such trademark counterfeiting is a contributing dimension of the larger problem of the proliferation of substandard, unsafe medicines. The United States notes its particular concern with the proliferation of counterfeit pharmaceuticals that are manufactured, sold, and distributed in trading partners such as **Brazil, China, Guatemala,**

India, Indonesia, Lebanon, Peru, and **Russia**. While it is impossible to determine an exact figure, studies have suggested that up to 20 percent of drugs sold in the Indian market are counterfeit and could represent a serious threat to patient health and safety. The U.S. Government, through the United States Agency for International Development (USAID) and other Federal agencies, supports programs in sub Saharan Africa, Asia, and elsewhere that assist trading partners in protecting the public against counterfeit and also substandard medicines (medicines that do not conform to established quality standards) introduced into their markets. Ninety seven percent of all counterfeit pharmaceuticals seized at the U.S. border in Fiscal Year 2015 were shipped from four economies: **China, Hong Kong, India**, and **Singapore**.

The United States welcomes reports that certain governmental authorities have increased their vigilance against these dangerous products. For example, in 2015, customs authorities in **Hong Kong** reportedly increased their efforts to seize counterfeit pharmaceuticals. Additionally, in September 2015, CBP collaborated with **Singapore** Customs to conduct a joint enforcement operation that focused on addressing the issue of counterfeit pharmaceuticals.

Many countries do not provide penalties that deter criminal enterprises engaged in global trademark counterfeiting operations. Even when such enterprises are investigated and prosecuted, the penalties imposed on them in many countries are low. Rather than deter further infringements, such penalties merely add to the cost of doing business.

Online sales of counterfeit goods have the potential to surpass the volume of sales through traditional channels such as street vendors and other physical markets. Enforcement authorities, unfortunately, face difficulties in responding to this trend (See *2015 Notorious Markets List* for more information on "Emerging Marketing and Distribution Tactics in Internet Facilitated Counterfeiting"). Counterfeiters increasingly continue to use legitimate express mail, international courier, and postal services to deliver counterfeit goods in small consignments rather than ocean going cargo, to make it more challenging for enforcement officials to interdict these goods. Counterfeiters also continue to ship products separately from counterfeit labels and packaging to evade enforcement efforts that target, or are limited by laws that require, the counterfeit item to be "completed" which may overlook the downstream application of counterfeit labels.[2]

The United States continues to urge trading partners to undertake more effective criminal and border enforcement against the manufacture, import, export, transit, and distribution of counterfeit goods. USTR engages with its trading partners through bilateral consultations, trade agreements, and international organizations to help ensure that penalties, such as significant monetary fines and meaningful sentences of imprisonment, are available and applied so as to have a deterrent effect on counterfeiting. In addition, trading partners should ensure that both counterfeit goods, as well as the materials and implements used for their production, are seized and destroyed, and thereby removed from the channels of commerce. Permitting counterfeit goods and enabling materials to reenter the channels of commerce after an enforcement action wastes resources and compromises the global enforcement effort. Trading partners should also provide enforcement officials with the authority to seize suspect goods and destroy counterfeit goods in country and at the border during import or export, or in transit movement, ex officio, without the need for a formal complaint from a right holder.

The U.S. Government coordinates with and supports trading partners through technical assistance and sharing of best practices on criminal and border enforcement, including with respect to the destruction of seized goods (See **ANNEX 2**). For example, CBP is interested in exploring opportunities for tangible cooperation on, among other issues, the border enforcement issues

---

[2] For more information on these trends and CBP's and ICE/HIS's IPR enforcement efforts, see Department of Homeland Security, Intellectual Property Rights Seizure Statistics, Fiscal Year 2015 (2015) available at https://www.cbp.gov/sites/default/files/assets/documents/2016-Apr/FY%202015%20IPR%20Stats%20Presentation.pdf

highlighted above. These opportunities could include sharing best practices and customs to customs information exchange for use in risk management and enforcement actions, as well as conducting joint customs enforcement operations designed to interdict shipment of IPR infringing goods destined for the United States. In addition, CBP is interested in pursuing bilateral and multilateral engagement on the role of the Internet and mobile technologies in the facilitation and proliferation of counterfeit and pirated goods.

Trademark Protection Issues

Trademarks help consumers distinguish providers of products and services from each other and thereby serve a critical source identification role. The goodwill represented in a company's trademark is often one of the company's most valuable business assets.

However, in numerous countries, legal and procedural obstacles exist to securing trademark rights. Many countries need to establish or improve transparency and consistency in their administrative trademark registration procedures. For example, the trademark system in **China** suffers from a high level of formalities required to bring opposition actions, inflexibility in relation to descriptions of goods/services, disregard for affidavits and witness declarations in inter partes proceedings, unreasonably high standards for establishing "well known" mark status, and lack of transparency in all phases of trademark prosecution.

Many other countries, including **Argentina, Brazil, India, Malaysia, Mexico, Panama, the Philippines**, and **Russia** reportedly either have no administrative opposition proceeding, an extremely limited opposition proceeding, or extremely delayed opposition proceedings.

Mandatory requirements to record trademark licenses are another concern, as they frequently impose unnecessary burdens, both administrative and financial, on trademark owners and create difficulty in the enforcement and maintenance of trademark rights. The absence of adequate means for searching trademark applications and registrations, such as by online databases, makes obtaining trademark protection more complicated and unpredictable. More than 30 nations, including **Argentina, Brazil, Egypt, Indonesia, Thailand**, and the **United Arab Emirates** require single Class trademark applications. Such systems lead to additional cost, both in terms of initial filing and in relation to docketing and maintenance of multiple registrations.

Also, in a number of countries, governments often do not provide the full range of internationally recognized trademark protections. For example, dozens of countries do not offer a certification mark system for use by foreign or domestic industries. The lack of a certification mark system can make it more difficult to secure protection for products with a quality or characteristic that consumers associate with the product's geographic origin. Robust protection for well known marks is also important for many U.S. producers and traders who have built up the reputation of their brands.

Trademark Protection Challenges in Country Code Top-Level Domain Names

Trademark holders continue to face challenges in protecting their trademarks against unauthorized uses in country code top level domain names (ccTLDs). U.S. right holders face significant trademark infringement and loss of valuable Internet traffic because of such uses, and it is important for countries to provide for appropriate remedies in their legal systems to address this issue. Many ccTLDs have policies that prohibit cybersquatting; require that the domain name have a nexus to the relevant country (e.g., citizenship or residency, a registered office, or a bona fide presence); require the registrant to provide true and complete contact information; and make such registration information publicly available or cooperate with brand owners whose trade marks are being infringed. The ccTLDs in **China, Denmark, Germany, The Netherlands, Spain, Sweden**, and **Switzerland** have been identified by right holders as ineffective or uncooperative. A related and growing concern is that some ccTLDs lack transparent and predictable domain name dispute resolution policies. Such effective policies should assist in the quick and efficient resolution of trademark infringement related domain name disputes. The United States encourages its trading partners to provide procedures that allow for the protection of trademarks used in domain names and to ensure that dispute resolution procedures are available to prevent the misuse of trademarks.

Government Use of Unlicensed Software

According to a 2014 study by BSA | The Software Alliance, the commercial value of unlicensed software globally is at least $62 billion.[3] USTR has undertaken an initiative to work with other governments, particularly in countries that are modernizing their software systems or where concerns have been raised, against unauthorized government use of software. Considerable progress has been made under this initiative, leading to numerous trading partners' mandating that only legitimate software be used by their government bodies. It is important for governments to legitimize their own activities in order to set an example of respecting IPR for private enterprises. Further work on this issue remains with certain trading partners, such as **China, Macedonia, Pakistan, Panama, Paraguay, South Korea, Taiwan, Tajikistan, Thailand, Turkmenistan, Ukraine,** and **Vietnam**. The United States urges trading partners to adopt and implement effective and transparent procedures to ensure legitimate governmental use of software.

Digital Piracy, Piracy Online, and Broadcast Piracy

The increased availability of broadband Internet connections around the world, combined with increasingly accessible and sophisticated mobile technology, is generating significant benefits, ranging from economic activity based on new business models to greater access to information. However, these technological developments have also made the Internet an extremely efficient vehicle for disseminating infringing content and for supplanting legitimate opportunities for copyright holders and online platforms that deliver licensed content. The U.S. Government's 2015 Notorious Markets List includes examples of online marketplaces reportedly engaging in commercial scale piracy online, including sites hosted in, operated by, or directed toward parties located in **Brazil, Canada, China, India, Russia, Switzerland, Ukraine**, and elsewhere.

While optical disc piracy continues in many countries, including in **China, India, Paraguay**, and **Vietnam**, piracy over the Internet has become the most challenging copyright enforcement issue in many trading partner markets. For example, "camcorded" copies (i.e., unauthorized recordings made in movie theaters) of first run motion pictures that are distributed worldwide via the Internet result in economic harm not only in the market where the film was originally shown, but in many other markets as well. Other examples of Internet enabled piracy found in virtually every country on the Special 301 lists include: the unauthorized retransmission of live sports programming over the Internet; pirate servers or "grey shards" that allow users to play unauthorized versions of cloud based entertainment software; online distribution of software and devices that allow for the circumvention of TPMs, including "game copiers" and mod chips that allow users to play pirated games on physical consoles; and set top or media boxes preloaded with large vol

---

[3] 2014 BSA Global Software Survey, available at http://globalstudy.bsa.org/2013/downloads/studies/2013GlobalSurvey_Study_en.pdf

umes of pirated content or configured with apps to facilitate access to infringing websites. Piracy facilitated by Internet based services present unique enforcement challenges for right holders in countries where copyright laws have not been able to adapt or keep pace with these innovations in piracy.

The availability of, and recourse by right holders to, enforcement procedures and remedies is a critical component of the online ecosystem. However, governments must also play a role, particularly in situations of online piracy that implicate multiple jurisdictions. Governments should avoid creating a domestic environment that offers a safe haven for piracy on the Internet.

For example, the United States urges **Hong Kong** to address rampant online piracy at the earliest opportunity. Hong Kong's failure to address this major problem represents a growing concern in what is otherwise generally a positive environment for IPR protection and enforcement.

Trade Secrets

This year's Report continues to reflect a growing need for trading partners to provide effective protection and enforcement of trade secrets. Companies in a wide variety of industry sectors, including information and communications technologies, services, biopharmaceuticals, manufacturing, and environmental technologies, rely on the ability to protect and enforce their trade secrets and rights in other proprietary information. Indeed, trade secrets, such as business plans, internal market analysis, manufacturing methods, customer lists, and recipes, are often among a company's core business assets; and a company's competitiveness may depend on its capacity to protect such assets. Trade secret theft threatens to diminish U.S. competitiveness around the globe, and puts U.S. jobs at risk. The reach of trade secret theft into critical commercial and defense technologies poses threats to U.S. national security interests as well.

Various sources, including the U.S. Office of the National Counterintelligence Executive (ONCIX), have reported specific gaps in trade secret protection and enforcement, particularly in **China**. The ONCIX publication titled *Foreign Spies Stealing U.S. Economic Secrets in Cyberspace*, states that "Chinese actors are the world's most active and persistent perpetrators of economic espionage." Theft may arise in a variety of circumstances, including those involving departing employees taking portable storage devices containing trade secrets, failed joint ventures, cyber intrusion and hacking, and misuse of information submitted by trade secret owners to government entities for purposes of complying with regulatory obligations. In practice, effective remedies appear to be difficult to obtain in a number of countries, including in **China** and **India**. Lack of legal certainty regarding trade secrets dissuades companies from entering into partnerships or expanding their business activities in these and other countries. Many countries do not provide criminal penalties for trade secret theft sufficient to deter such behavior. Some foreign countries' practices and policies put valuable trade secrets at risk of exposure including evidentiary requirements in trade secrets litigation and mandatory technology transfer. For example, in **Brazil, Indonesia**, and **Nigeria** government procurement regulations may require companies to disclose valuable source code.

The United States uses all trade tools available to ensure that its trading partners provide robust protection for trade secrets and enforce trade secrets laws. The 2013 [Administration Strategy on Mitigating the Theft of U.S. Trade Secrets](#) from the U.S. Intellectual Property Enforcement Coordinator (IPEC) continues to guide U.S. government efforts to combat the theft of trade secrets that could be used by foreign governments or companies to gain an unfair commercial and economic advantage

Given the global nature of trade secret theft, action by our trading partners is essential. Several trading partners have been working toward strengthening their trade secret regimes, including **China**, the **EU**, **Kazakhstan**, and **Taiwan**.

Action in international organizations is also critical. For instance, the United States strongly supports continued work in the **OECD** on trade secret protection, building off of the two studies released by the OECD in 2014. The first study, entitled "Approaches to Protection of Undisclosed Information (Trade Secrets)" (January 30, 2014), surveyed legal protection for trade secrets available in a sample of countries. The second study, entitled "Uncovering Trade Secrets An Empirical Assessment of Economic Implications of Protection for Undisclosed Data" (August 11, 2014), examined the protection of trade secrets for a sample of 37 countries, provided historical data for the period since 1985, and considered the relationship between the stringency of trade secret protection and relevant economic performance indicators.

Localization, Indigenous Innovation, and Forced Technology Transfer

Right holders operating in other countries report an increasing variety of government measures, policies, and practices that are touted as means to incentivize domestic "indigenous innovation," but that, in practice, can disadvantage U.S. companies, such as by requiring foreign companies to give up their IPR as the price of market entry. Such initiatives serve as market access barriers, discouraging foreign investment and hurting local manufacturers, distributors, and retailers. Such government imposed conditions or incentives may distort licensing and other private business arrangements, resulting in commercially suboptimal outcomes for the firms involved and for in novation, generally. Further, these measures discourage foreign investment in national econo mies, slowing the pace of innovation and economic progress. Government intervention in the commercial decisions that enterprises make regarding the ownership, development, registration, or licensing of IPR is not consistent with international practice, and may raise concerns regarding consistency with international obligations as well.

These government measures often have the effect of distorting trade by forcing U.S. compa nies to transfer their technology or other valuable commercial information to national entities. Examples of these policies include:

- Requiring the transfer of technology as a condition for obtaining regulatory approvals or oth erwise securing access to a market, or for allowing a company to continue to do business in the market;

- Directing SOEs in innovative sectors to seek non commercial terms from their foreign busi ness partners, including with respect to the acquisition and use or licensing of IPR;

- Providing national firms with a competitive advantage by failing to effectively enforce for eign held IPR, including patents, trademarks, trade secrets, and copyrights;

- Failing to take meaningful measures to prevent or deter cyber intrusions and other unauthor ized activities;

- Requiring use of, or providing preferences to, products or services that contain locally devel oped or owned IPR or that are produced by local manufactures or service providers, including with respect to government procurements;

- Manipulating the standards development process to create unfair advantages for national firms, including with respect to the terms on which IPR is licensed; and

- Requiring the (often unnecessary) submission of excessive confidential business information for regulatory approval purposes and failing to protect such information appropriately.

In **China**, market access, government procurement, and the receipt of certain preferences or benefits are conditioned on a firm's ability to demonstrate that certain IPR is developed in China or is owned by or licensed, in some cases exclusively, to a Chinese party. In **India**, in country testing requirements and data and server localization requirements are frequently cited by U.S. industry as inhibiting market access and blunting innovation in the information and communications technology sector. In **Indonesia**, it is reported that foreign companies' approvals to market pharmaceuticals are conditioned upon the transfer of technology to Indonesian entities or upon partial manufacture in Indonesia. In **Nigeria**, the United States is concerned about localization policies that appear to be aimed at protecting and favoring local companies at the expense of foreign firms, investors, and multinational enterprises. In particular, the 2013 *Guidelines for Nigerian Content Development in Information and Communications Technology* (ICT) require local production or utilization of Nigerian material and labor across a broad range of ICT goods and services. Requirements of particular concern are server localization mandates (e.g., requirements for domestic production and utilization of nationally developed technology), cross border data flow restrictions, programs to support only local data hosting firms, and aspects that overtly impose burdens on foreign firms by requiring in country R&D departments and disclosure of source code and other proprietary information. Other country specific examples of these measures are identified in **Section II**.

The United States urges that, in formulating policies to promote innovation, trading partners, including China and India, take account of the increasingly cross border nature of commercial R&D and technology supply chains, and of the importance of voluntary and mutually agreed commercial partnerships.

Market Access and Pharmaceutical and Medical Device Innovation

Among other mechanisms to support pharmaceutical and medical device innovation, USTR has sought to reduce market access barriers, including those that discriminate against U.S. companies, are not adequately transparent, or do not offer sufficient opportunity for meaningful stakeholder engagement, in order to facilitate both affordable health care today and the innovation that assures improved health care tomorrow. This year's Report highlights concerns regarding market access barriers affecting U.S. persons that rely on IPR protection, including those in the pharmaceutical and medical device industries, particularly in **Algeria, India**, and **Indonesia**.

Measures, including those that are discriminatory, nontransparent or otherwise trade restrictive, have the potential to hinder market access in the pharmaceutical and medical device sector, and potentially result in higher healthcare costs. For example, taxes or tariffs may be levied often in a non transparent manner on imported medicines, and the increased expense associated with those levies is then passed directly to healthcare institutions and patients. By some estimates, federal and state taxes can add 38 percent to the cost of medicines in **Brazil** and according to an October 2012 WTO report titled *More Trade for Better Health? International Trade and Tariffs on Health Products*, **India** maintains the highest tariffs on medicines, pharmaceutical inputs, and medical devices among the WTO members identified in the report. These tariffs, combined with domestic charges or measures, particularly those that lack transparency or opportunities for meaningful stakeholder engagement or that appear to exempt domestically developed and manufactured medicines, can hinder government efforts to promote increased access to health care products.

Moreover, unreasonable regulatory approval delays and non transparent reimbursement policies can impede a company's ability to enter the market, and thereby discourage the development and marketing of new drugs and other medical products. The criteria, rationale, and operation of such measures are often nontransparent or not fully disclosed to patients or to pharmaceutical and medical device companies seeking to market their products. USTR encourages trading partners to provide appropriate mechanisms for transparency, procedural and due process protections, and opportunities for public engagement in the context of their relevant health care systems.

The U.S. pharmaceutical and medical device industry has expressed concerns regarding the policies of several trading partners, including **Algeria, Austria, Belgium, China, Colombia, Czech Republic, Ecuador, Hungary, Italy, Korea, Lithuania, New Zealand, Portugal, Romania, Taiwan**, and **Turkey**, on issues related to pharmaceutical innovation and market access. Examples of these concerns include:

- A ban in **Algeria** on more than 350 imported pharmaceutical products and medical devices in favor of local products is a trade matter of paramount concern and is the primary reason why Algeria remains on the Priority Watch List. The United States urges Algeria to remove this market access barrier that is also reportedly adversely affecting access to legitimate medicines;

- The lack of efficiency, transparency, and fairness in the pharmaceutical manufacturing inspection process in **Turkey**;

- A series of measures in several **EU** Member States, including **Austria, Belgium, Czech Republic, Finland, Hungary, Italy, Lithuania, Portugal**, and **Romania** that raise concerns with respect to the transparency and the opportunity for meaningful stakeholder engagement in policies related to pricing and reimbursement, which reportedly create uncertainty and unpredictability that adversely impact market access and incentives for further innovation;

- Proposals in **Colombia** and **Ecuador** designed to enhance domestic manufacturing capacity for pharmaceuticals that could adversely affect market entry and investment and, in effect, limit access by consumers to the latest generation of medicines; and

- Policies and the operation of **New Zealand**'s Pharmaceutical Management Agency (PHARMAC), which include, among other things, the lack of transparency, fairness, and predictability of the PHARMAC pricing and reimbursement regime, as well as negative aspects of the overall climate for innovative medicines in New Zealand.

The United States seeks to establish, or continue, dialogues with trading partners to address these and other concerns and to encourage a common understanding on questions related to innovation in the pharmaceutical and medical device sectors. The United States also looks forward to continuing its engagement with our trading partners to promote fair and transparent policies in this sector.

The United States, like many countries, faces healthcare challenges, including with respect to aging populations and rising health care costs. The United States shares the objectives of continuing improvement in the health and quality of life of its citizens, and of delivering efficient, responsive, and cost effective, high quality health care to its population. The United States looks forward to engaging with its trading partners on the concerns noted above.

Geographical Indications

The United States is working intensively through bilateral and multilateral channels to advance U.S. market access interests and to ensure that the trade initiatives of the **EU** and its Member

States in other countries and international organizations, including with respect to GI protection, do not undercut U.S. industries' market access. GIs typically include place names (or words associated with a place) and they identify products or services as having a particular quality, reputation, or other characteristic essentially attributable by consumers in the territory of protection to the geographic origin of the product or service. The EU GI agenda remains highly concerning in two key respects — in terms of the significant extent to which it undermines the scope of other IPRs, particularly trademarks, held by U.S. producers, and concomitantly imposes barriers to market access for American made goods and services that rely on the scope of such rights.

First, the EU GI system raises concerns regarding the extent to which it impairs the scope of trademark protection, which remains among the most effective ways for companies, including SMEs, to create value, promote their goods and services, and protect their brands, including with respect to food and beverage products covered by the EU GI system. Many such products are already protected in the United States, in the EU, and around the world by trademarks. Trademark systems offer strong protections through procedures that are easy to use, cost effective, and transparent and that provide due process safeguards as well as high consumer awareness, significant contributions to national GDPs and employment, and long recognized international systems of protection.

Second, the troubling aspects of the EU GI system, in turn, result in negative market impacts for U.S. and other producers in the EU market. For example, United States EU trade in agricultural products is highly asymmetrical, with the United States running a significant trade deficit. In the case of cheese, for example, the EU exports nearly $1 billion of cheese to the United States each year; the United States exports only about $6 million to the EU. Conversely, EU agricultural producers exporting to the United States are doing quite well, benefiting considerably from the scope of trademark protection provided in the United States, and notably in the absence of an EU style GI system.

Despite these troubling aspects of its GI system, the EU continues to seek to expand its system within its territory and beyond. Within its borders, the EU is progressing toward enlarging its system beyond agricultural products and foodstuffs, to non agricultural products, including apparel, ceramics, glass, handicrafts, manufactured goods, minerals, salts, stones, and textiles. Beyond its borders, the EU has sought to advance its agenda through bilateral trade agreements, which extend the negative market impacts of the EU GI system on the scope of trademark protection to third countries.

The same is true in the multilateral context. For example, culminating in May of 2015, the EU and several of its Member States expanded the WIPO Lisbon Agreement for the Protection of Appellations of Origin and their International Registration to include GIs, thereby enshrining several detrimental aspects of EU law in this Agreement. The Geneva Act of the Lisbon Agreement that emerged from these negotiations resulted from a decision taken by the EU and those Member States to break with the long standing WIPO practice of consensus and to vote to deny the United States and 160 other WIPO countries of meaningful participation rights in the negotiations.

In response, the United States continues its intensive engagement in promoting and protecting access to foreign markets for U.S. exporters whose products are trademark protected or are identified by common names like parmesan and feta for cheese. The United States is advancing these objectives intensively through its free trade agreements, such as the TPP and T TIP, as well as in international fora, including in APEC, WIPO, and the WTO. In addition to these negotiations, the United States is also engaging bilaterally to address GI related concerns resulting from the GI provisions of EU trade agreements and other initiatives, including with **Canada, China, Costa Rica, El Salvador, Japan, Jordan, Morocco, the Philippines, South Africa**, and **Vietnam**, among others. U.S. goals in this regard include:

- Ensuring that the grant of GI protection does not violate prior rights (for example, in cases in which a U.S. company has a trademark that includes a place name);

- Ensuring that the grant of GI protection does not deprive interested parties of the ability to use common names, such as parmesan or feta;

- Ensuring that interested persons have notice of, and opportunity to oppose or to seek cancellation of, any GI protection that is sought or granted;

- Ensuring that notices issued when granting a GI consisting of compound terms identify its common name components; and

- Opposing efforts to extend the protection given to GIs for wines and spirits to other products.

Other Issues

Some public comments received in response to the 2016 Special 301 *Federal Register* notice also identified developments in several countries that may have created market uncertainties for technology companies and online content providers such as laws that involve remuneration by news aggregation services providers. The United States is monitoring these developments and other related measures. (See Fact Sheet: Key Barriers to Digital Trade). USTR detailed this and many other issues in the 2016 National Trade Estimate Report.

Intellectual Property and the Environment

Strong IPR protection and enforcement are essential to promoting investment in innovation in the environmental sector. Such innovation not only promotes economic growth and supports jobs, but also is critical to responding to environmental challenges. IPR provides incentives for R&D in this important sector, including through university research. Conversely, inadequate IPR protection and enforcement in foreign markets discourages entry into technology transfer arrangements and broader investment in those markets. This may hinder the realization of not just technological advances needed to meet environmental challenges, including the mitigation of, and adaptation to, climate change, but also regional economic growth, as a whole.

Certain national policies and practices advanced domestically and in multilateral fora may have the effect of undermining innovation needed to address serious environmental challenges. For example, India's National Manufacturing Policy promotes the compulsory licensing of patented technologies as a means of effectuating technology transfer with respect to green technologies. Such policies, which India has sought to multilateralize in United Nations (UN) negotiations, will discourage, rather than promote, investment in and dissemination of green technology innovation, including those technologies that contribute to climate change adaptation and mitigation.

Significantly, the Parties to the UN Framework Convention on Climate Change (UNFCCC), including the United States, succeeded in enshrining the critical role of technological innovation in the context of climate change in the recently concluded Paris Agreement. Article 10(5) of the Paris Agreement provides, "Accelerating, encouraging and enabling innovation is critical for an effective, long term global response to climate change and promoting economic growth and sustainable development." This provision provides a strong model for future work on this issue. As part of these negotiations, the United States and numerous other UNFCCC Members continued to maintain the strong and positive relationship between IPR protection and enforcement and green technology innovation, which was reflected in the fact that all negative references to IPR were removed from the final text of the Paris Agreement and accompanying decision, which were contained in early proposals from certain UNFCCC Members.

Intellectual Property and Health

Numerous comments in the 2016 Special 301 review process highlighted concerns arising at the intersection of IPR policy and health policy. IPR protection plays an important role in providing the incentives necessary for the development and marketing of new medicines. An effective, transparent, and predictable IPR system is necessary for both manufacturers of innovative medicines and manufacturers of generic medicines.

The 2001 WTO Doha Declaration on the TRIPS Agreement and Public Health recognized the gravity of the public health problems afflicting many developing and least developed countries, especially those resulting from HIV/AIDS, tuberculosis, malaria, and other epidemics. As affirmed in the Doha Declaration on the TRIPS Agreement and Public Health, the United States respects a trading partner's right to protect public health and, in particular, to promote access to medicines for all. The United States also recognizes the role of IPR protection in the development of new medicines, while being mindful of the effect of IPR protection on prices. The assessments set forth in this Report are based on various critical factors, including, where relevant, the Doha Declaration on the TRIPS Agreement and Public Health.

The United States is firmly of the view that international obligations such as those in the TRIPS Agreement have sufficient flexibility to allow trading partners to address the serious public health problems that they may face. Consistent with this view, the United States respects its trading partners' rights to grant compulsory licenses in a manner consistent with the provisions of the TRIPS Agreement and the Doha Declaration on the TRIPS Agreement and Public Health, and encourages its trading partners to consider ways to address their public health challenges while also maintaining IPR systems that promote innovation.

The United States also strongly supports the WTO General Council Decision on the Implementation of Paragraph 6 of the Doha Declaration on the TRIPS Agreement and Public Health concluded in August 2003. Under this decision, WTO Members are permitted, in accordance with specified procedures, to issue compulsory licenses to export pharmaceutical products to countries that cannot produce drugs for themselves. The WTO General Council adopted a Decision in December 2005 that incorporated this solution into an amendment to the TRIPS Agreement, and the United States became the first WTO Member to formally accept this amendment. The United States encourages other WTO members to accept this amendment by the current deadline, December 31, 2017. If two thirds of WTO members accept the amendment, it will go into effect for those Members. The August 2003 waiver will remain in place and be available until the amendment takes effect.

The U.S. Government works to ensure that the provisions of its bilateral and regional trade agreements, as well as U.S. engagement in international organizations, including the UN and related institutions such as WIPO and the WHO, are consistent with U.S. policies concerning IPR and health policy and do not impede its trading partners from taking measures necessary to protect public health. Accordingly, USTR will continue its close cooperation with relevant agencies to ensure that public health challenges are addressed and IPR protection and enforcement are supported as one of various mechanisms to promote research and innovation.

Implementation of the WTO TRIPS Agreement

The TRIPS Agreement, one of the most significant achievements of the Uruguay Round (1986 1994), requires all WTO Members to provide certain minimum standards of IPR protection and enforcement. The TRIPS Agreement is the first broadly subscribed multilateral IPR agreement that is subject to mandatory dispute settlement provisions.

Developed country WTO Members were required to implement the TRIPS Agreement fully as of January 1, 1996. Developing country Members were given a transition period for many obligations until January 1, 2000, and in some cases, until January 1, 2005. Nevertheless, certain Members are still in the process of finalizing implementing legislation, and many are still engaged in establishing adequate and effective IPR enforcement mechanisms.

Recognizing the particular challenges faced by WTO Members that are least developed countries (LDC), the United States has worked closely with them and other WTO Members to extend the implementation date for these countries. For example, on November 6, 2015, the TRIPS Council reached consensus to extend the transition period for LDC Members to implement Sections 5 and 7 of the TRIPS Agreement with respect to pharmaceutical products until January 1, 2033, and reached consensus to recommend waiving Articles 70.8 and 70.9 of the TRIPS Agreement with respect to pharmaceuticals also until January 1, 2033, which the WTO General Council adopted on November 30, 2015. Likewise, on June 11, 2013, the TRIPS Council reached consensus on a decision to again extend the transition period under Article 66.1 of the TRIPS Agreement for LDC WTO Members. Under this decision, LDC WTO Members are not required to apply the provisions of the TRIPS Agreement, other than Articles 3, 4, and 5 (provisions related to national treatment and most favored nation treatment), until July 1, 2021, or until such a date on which they cease to be an LDC WTO Member, whichever date is earlier.

On November 23, 2015, the TRIPS Council reached agreement to extend the moratorium on non violation and situation complaints under the TRIPS Agreement until the next Ministerial in 2017. The moratorium was originally introduced in Article 64 of the TRIPS Agreement, for a period of five years following the entry into force of the WTO Agreement (i.e., until December 31, 1999). The moratorium has been referred to and extended in several WTO Ministerial documents, most recently in 2013. In 2015, the TRIPS Council intensified its discussions on this issue, including on the basis of a communication by the United States to the Council outlining the U.S. position on non violation and situation complaints. This communication (document number IP/C/W/599) addressed the relevant TRIPS Agreement provisions, WTO and GATT disputes, and provided responses to issues raised by other WTO Members.

The United States participates actively in the WTO TRIPS Council's scheduled reviews of WTO Members' implementation of the TRIPS Agreement, and also uses the WTO's Trade Policy Review mechanism to pose questions and seek constructive engagement on issues related to TRIPS Agreement implementation.

Dispute Settlement and Enforcement

The United States continues to monitor the resolution of disputes announced in previous Special 301 Reports. The most efficient and preferred manner of resolving concerns is through bilateral dialogue. Some of the positive developments identified in this Report are evidence of successful dialogue. Where these bilateral efforts are unsuccessful, the United States will use enforcement tools including the WTO and other dispute settlement procedures, as appropriate.

In April 2007, the United States initiated dispute settlement procedures relating to deficien cies in China's legal regime for protecting and enforcing copyrights and trademarks on a wide range of products. In March 2009, the WTO Dispute Settlement Body (DSB) adopted a panel report that upheld two of the claims advanced by the United States, finding that: (1) China's denial of copyright protection to works that do not meet China's content review standards is impermissible under the TRIPS Agreement; and (2) China's customs rules cannot allow seized counterfeit goods to be publicly auctioned after only removing the spurious trademark. With respect to a third claim concerning China's thresholds for criminal prosecution and conviction of counterfeiting and piracy, while the United States prevailed on the interpretation of the important legal standards in Article 61 of the TRIPS Agreement, including the finding that criminal enforcement measures must reflect and respond to the realities of the commercial marketplace, the panel found that it needed additional evidence before it could uphold the overall U.S. claim that China's criminal thresholds are too high. On March 19, 2010, China announced that it had completed all the necessary domestic legislative procedures to implement the DSB recommendations and rulings. The United States continues to monitor China's implementation of the DSB recommendations and rulings in this dispute.

In addition, the United States requested WTO dispute settlement consultations with China concerning certain other Chinese measures affecting market access and distribution for imported publications, movies, and music, and audio visual home entertainment products (e.g., DVDs and Blu ray discs) (AVHE products). The U.S. claims challenged China's prohibition on foreign companies' importation of all products at issue; China's prohibitions and discriminatory requirements imposed on foreign distributors of publications, music, and AVHE products within China; and China's imposition of more burdensome requirements on the distribution of imported publications, movies, and music vis à vis their domestic counterparts. On January 19, 2010, the DSB adopted panel and Appellate Body reports that found in favor of the United States on the vast majority of its claims. China committed to bring all relevant measures into compliance with the DSB recommendations by March 19, 2011, and subsequently revised or revoked measures relating to publications, AVHE products, and music. China did not issue any measures relating to theatrical films, but instead proposed bilateral discussions. In February 2012, the United States and China reached an agreement on the terms of an MOU that provides significantly increased market access for imported films and significantly improved compensation for foreign film producers. The United States continues to review and monitor the steps that China has taken toward compliance in this matter.

Following the 1999 Special 301 review process, the United States initiated dispute settlement consultations concerning the EU regulation on food related GIs, which appeared to discriminate against foreign products and persons, notably by requiring that EU trading partners adopt an "EU style" system of GI protection, and appeared to provide insufficient protections to trademark owners. On April 20, 2005, the DSB adopted a panel report finding in favor of the United States that the EU GI regulation is inconsistent with the EU's obligations under the TRIPS Agreement and the General Agreement on Tariffs and Trade 1994. On March 31, 2006, the EU published a revised GI Regulation that is intended to comply with the DSB recommendations and rulings. There remain some concerns, however, with respect to this revised GI Regulation, which the United States has asked the EU to address. The United States intends to continue monitoring this situation. The United States is also working intensively bilaterally and in multilateral fora to advance U.S. market access interests, and to ensure that the trade initiatives of other countries, including with respect to GIs, do not undercut market access for U.S. companies.

SECTION II
Country Reports

Priority Watch List

EAST ASIA AND THE PACIFIC

CHINA

China remains on the Priority Watch List and subject to Section 306 monitoring in 2016.

China continues to present a complex and contradictory environment for protection and enforcement of IPR. Welcome developments include repeated affirmation of the importance of intellectual property by China's leadership, an ongoing intellectual property legal and regulatory reform effort, and encouraging developments in individual cases in China's courts. At the same time, progress toward effective protection and enforcement of IPR in China is undermined by unchecked trade secret theft, market access obstacles to ICT products raised in the name of security, measures favoring domestically owned intellectual property in the name of promoting innovation in China, rampant piracy and counterfeiting in China's massive online and physical markets, extensive use of unlicensed software, and the supply of counterfeit goods to foreign markets. Additional challenges arise in the form of obstacles that restrict foreign firms' ability to fully participate in standards setting, the unnecessary introduction of inapposite competition concepts into intellectual property laws, and acute challenges in protecting and incentivizing the creation of pharmaceutical inventions and test data. As a result, surveys continue to show that the uncertain intellectual property environment is a leading concern for businesses operating in China, as intellectual property infringements are difficult to prevent and remediate, and may cause businesses to choose not to invest in China or offer their technology, goods, or services there. Despite these concerns, the United States welcomes the commitment of China's leadership to intellectual property and innovation, and urges it to seize the opportunity of ongoing legal and regulatory reform to translate policy commitments into an intellectual property environment in China that provides for effective IPR protection and enforcement, incentivizes innovation, and facilitates trade in IPR intensive goods and services.

High Level Commitments and Wide-Ranging Legal Reform

In 2015, China's leadership continued to affirm the importance of developing and protecting intellectual property and emphasized that stronger protection and enforcement of IPR are essential to achieving China's economic objectives. China expressly committed not to "conduct or knowingly support misappropriation of intellectual property, including trade secrets and other confidential business information with the intent of providing competitive advantages to . . . [its] companies or commercial sectors." China also committed not to "require the transfer of intellectual property rights or technology as a condition of doing business . . . ." As part of its legal reform effort, China continued to develop draft measures on a wide range of subjects, including on copyright, patents, trade secrets, drug review and approvals, Anti Monopoly Law enforcement as it relates to intellectual property, and regulations on inventor remuneration. To date, the proposed reforms include many welcome changes but also aspects that are of great concern. China continues to review its Copyright Law, and revisions aligned with international norms and best practices would put China on a stronger footing to encourage growth in, and investment by, industries relying on copyright protection. Another positive development is that the Office of the National Leading Group on the Fight Against IPR Infringement and Counterfeiting, established by the State Council and chaired by Vice Premier Wang Yang, continues to play an important and positive role in intellectual property, and it extended its online enforcement campaign into 2015. Also welcome is China's three-year pilot program to study the merits of specialized intellectual property courts, currently including courts in Beijing, Shanghai, and Guangzhou.

Trade Secrets

Trade secret theft remains a serious and growing problem in China. (See **Trade Secrets**). Although the misappropriation of trade secrets and their use by a competing enterprise can have a devastating impact on a company's business, remedies can be exceedingly difficult to obtain under current Chinese law and insufficient to match the level of the threat. Enforcement obstacles include deficiencies in China's primary trade secrets law (found in the Anti-Unfair Competition Law, or AUCL) that limit the law's application; unresolved weaknesses in China's civil enforcement system including limited injunctive relief and low damage awards; and difficulties in pursuing criminal enforcement, including the need to prove actual damages caused by the theft of a trade secret. Without changes to address these limitations and weaknesses, some of which are not specific to intellectual property but relate to China's civil process generally, effective enforcement against misappropriation of trade secrets in China will remain challenging.

The United States welcomes China's effort to reform the AUCL, including through the release of draft amendments for comment that made notable progress in several areas. The revision to the AUCL presents an opportunity to address important obstacles, although other necessary changes fall outside the scope of the law in its present form. The United States urges China to consider drafting a stand-alone trade secrets law, which would provide an opportunity to address a broader range of concerns than possible as part of a reform to the AUCL. Other continuing concerns include the issue of misuse of confidential information submitted to Chinese authorities for regulatory purposes. In addition to engaging with China on the AUCL, the United States will also continue to work to ensure other important JCCT commitments are realized, including that "China...intends to issue model or guiding court cases; and intends to clarify rules on preliminary injunctions, evidence preservation orders and damages."

"Secure and Controllable" ICT Policies

Starting in 2014, a number of Chinese measures and draft measures have invoked security as a putative justification for mounting barriers to foreign ICT products and services and for requiring disclosure of critical intellectual property as a condition of access to the Chinese market. The troubling trend emerged in late 2014, when China issued a series of measures applying to banking sector purchases of ICT products and services. Collectively, the measures would over time require financial institutions operating in China to purchase an increasing share of ICT products, services, and technologies from suppliers whose IPR are indigenously Chinese. The rules also would require foreign firms to conduct ICT-related research and development (R&D) in China and to divulge proprietary intellectual property as a condition for the sale of ICT products and services in China. In response to strenuous objections from the United States, other foreign gov ernments, and the private sector, China suspended these measures in 2015, and at the 2015 JCCT meeting clarified that, as China solicits policy revision advice from concerned parties, the banking sector is free to purchase ICT products of their choosing, regardless of the country of origin of such products. These remedial actions are welcome, but they have not yet resulted in a rebound in sales of non Chinese ICT products and services to Chinese banks. An additional example of this unwelcome trend is China's draft counterterror law, which included provisions that appeared to require telecommunications business operators and Internet service providers to, among other things, disclose critical proprietary intellectual property to regulators. After the United States and others raised objections, China removed some of the most troubling provisions from the final version of the counterterror law. It is critical that these concepts not be reintroduced in implementing regulations or other measures. Similar concerns have arisen in China's National Security Law and draft insurance sector regulations. During President Xi's September 2015 visit to the United States, China committed that "generally applicable measures to enhance ICT cybersecurity in commercial sectors (ICT cybersecurity regulations) should be consistent with WTO agreements, be narrowly tailored, take into account international norms, be nondiscriminatory, and not impose nationality based conditions or restrictions, on the purchase, sale, or use of ICT products by commercial enterprises unnecessarily." Going forward, it is critical that China adhere to its commitments not to simply invoke security concerns in order to require the disclosure of critical intellectual property.

Technology Transfer Requirements and Incentives

Right holders in China must contend with government measures, policies, and practices that are purportedly intended to hasten China's development into an innovative economy, but that disadvantage foreign right holders. The United States is concerned about reports that many of China's innovation related policies and other industrial policies, such as strategic emerging industry policies, may have negative impacts on U.S. exports or U.S. investors and their investments or IPR. Chinese regulations, rules, and other measures frequently call for technology transfer and, in certain cases, appear to include criteria requiring that certain IPR be developed in China, or be owned by or licensed to, in some cases exclusively, a Chinese party. Such government intervention, including imposed conditions or incentives, may distort licensing and other private business arrangements, resulting in reduced innovation and a disincentive for relevant firms to participate in the Chinese market.

Through sustained bilateral engagement with China, the United States has secured commitments including that:

- "Technology transfer and technological cooperation shall be decided by businesses independently and will not be used by the Chinese government as a pre condition for market access";
- China must "treat intellectual property rights owned or developed in other countries the same as domestically owned or developed intellectual property rights"; and
- "Enterprises are free to base technology transfer decisions on business and market considerations, and are free to independently negotiate and decide whether and under what circumstances to assign or license intellectual property rights to affiliated or unaffiliated enterprises."

The United States looks forward to China's full implementation of its commitments, and the revision of measures as needed to ensure that they are consistent with such commitments, in cluding with respect to ICT and elements of the High and New Technology Enterprise tax incentive. At the same time, the United States will continue to push back against existing measures that distort technology transfer, including Regulations on Administration of Import and Export of Technologies, as well as new calls to localize foreign technology, such as by limiting certain regulatory incentives to those foreign pharmaceutical products that are produced in China.

Widespread Piracy and Counterfeiting in China's Massive E-Commerce Markets

Widespread online piracy and counterfeiting in China's massive e commerce markets result in great losses for U.S. right holders involved in the distribution of a wide array of trademarked products, as well as legitimate music, motion pictures, books and journals, video games, and software. Online piracy extends to unauthorized access to, or unauthorized copies of, scientific, technical, and medical publications as well. According to estimates, China has the largest Internet user base in the world, at around 650 million, with nearly 560 million mobile web users, and annual sales of goods of the Internet projected at nearly half a trillion U.S. dollars. In 2014, China's State Administration for Industry and Commerce (SAIC) reported that more than 40 percent of goods that SAIC purchased online during a survey were "not genuine," a classification that it described as including fakes. Although some leading online sales platforms have streamlined procedures to remove offerings of infringing articles, right holders report that the procedures are still burdensome and that repeat infringers are not deterred by penalties. Reports indicate that unauthorized camcording of movies in theaters, one of the primary sources for online audiovisual infringements, remains a serious problem in China. The United States urges China to accelerate the development of its E Commerce Law and to ensure that it addresses online piracy and counterfeiting, while providing appropriate safeguards to Internet service providers.

While these very substantial problems continue, right holders noted progress in enforcement against online piracy, particularly as to unlicensed music. In 2015, the National Copyright Administration of China (NCAC) ordered online music platforms to remove unlicensed works, resulting in declarations of compliance from various online platforms, the reported removal of over 2.2 million unlicensed works, the deletion of such works from 129 websites, and the closure of 42 websites. Right holders were also encouraged by an October 2015 notice from NCAC to service providers regarding unlicensed works. Right holders reported that ISPs are generally responsive to takedown notices and that right holder revenues increased in 2015 relative to 2014 but remain very low compared to a range of other markets, even after accounting for differences such as in population and gross domestic product.

Parties in China are facilitating online infringement, in China and third countries, through media box piracy. Manufactured in China and exported abroad, media boxes can be preloaded with infringing content or links to content sources and plugged directly into televisions. Industry reports that China is the home to the media box manufacturers and many of the servers that connect media box users to infringing content. These media boxes enable the users to stream and download infringing online music and audiovisual content. The vast majority of the infringing websites and third party apps to which media box users connect are also reportedly owned or operated by entities in China. Action by the State Administration of Press, Publication, Radio, Film and Television (SAPPRFT) reportedly led to the banning of 81 such apps in 2015. The United States applauds this action by SAPPRFT and urges appropriate action against the manufacturers of media boxes in the appropriate venue.

Regulations related to SAPPRFT review of foreign television content present a serious market access concern for the online distribution of imported films and television series. Legitimate vid eo streaming websites such as those operated by Sohu, Tencent, and others have represented an important gateway for U.S. and other foreign television content providers to reach consumers in China. The regulations have curtailed legitimate commerce through the imposition of a number of onerous registration requirements, while creating an incentive for consumers to search for content from unlicensed sources. The United States urges China to suspend the new regulations and to further consider the potential impacts of these far reaching regulatory changes.

Software Legalization

The United States continues to urge all levels of the Chinese government, as well as SOEs, to use only legitimate, licensed copies of software. China reported that from 2011 to 2014, software legalization was completed at government offices of all levels. Despite this effort, industry reported that in 2013, the commercial value of unlicensed software in China stood at almost $8.8 billion. In 2014, inspection teams dispatched by the Inter Ministerial Joint Conference on Promoting Use of Authorized Software Inspections identified problems among local governments, including the continued use of unauthorized software and incomplete implementation of software asset management tools. Despite China's attention to the concern, U.S. software companies have seen only a modest increase in sales to government agencies. China should provide specific information about the relevant procedures and tools used to ascertain budget and audit information.

While software legalization efforts have extended to China's SOE sector, losses by software companies due to piracy at SOEs and other enterprises remain very high. To the extent that Chinese firms do not pay for the software that runs many of their operations, they reap a cost advantage relative to competitors who pay for legally acquired software. The United States remains committed to working with China to continue to address these challenges.

China Is a Global Source of Counterfeit Goods

USTR's *2015 Notorious Markets List* reported that China is the manufacturing hub of counterfeit products sold illicitly in markets around the world. Counterfeit goods produced in China that are shipped to the United States include: food and beverages; apparel, footwear, and accessories; consumer electronics, computers and networking equipment; entertainment and business software; batteries; chemicals; appliances; pharmaceuticals; auto parts; and other commodities. As described in **Border and Criminal Enforcement Against Counterfeiting**, the effects of these counterfeit goods go beyond lost sales volume and harm to the reputations of U.S. trademark owners. Counterfeit pharmaceuticals potentially threaten the health of consumers around the world, and faulty or substandard goods that enter the supply chains of U.S. and other manufacturers are dangerous as well. For example, higher defect and failure rates among counterfeit semiconductors may cause malfunctions in medical devices and vehicle safety and braking systems. In China, counterfeit pesticides and fertilizers present potential health hazards to agricultural workers and consumers.

During Fiscal Year 2015, products from China accounted for an estimated 52 percent of the total value of the IPR infringing products seized at U.S. ports. Products transshipped through, or designated as originating in, Hong Kong, many of which also were produced in China, accounted for an additional 35 percent of the estimated total value of seizures at U.S. ports. China is also the largest producing economy of counterfeits when relying on detailed analysis of EU seizure data.[4] The United States and China have committed to strengthened cooperation on IPR border enforcement.

As China implements the 2013 amendments to the Trademark Law, long standing concerns, such as bad faith trademark registration by Chinese applicants, onerous documentation requirements, and difficulty in obtaining "well known" trademark status create a negative impact for legitimate right holders, particularly those first filed outside of China. Further, changes to trademark opposition procedures have eliminated an appeal process and have resulted in longer windows for bad faith trademark registrants to use their marks before a decision is made in an invalidation proceeding. On geographical indications (GIs), the United States has welcomed important commitments made by China in 2014 and 2015 regarding China's rules and procedures concerning GIs registered under China's existing systems, as well as those registered pursuant to an international agreement, and has continued to work with China to ensure that U.S. products with generic terms do not face displacement in the Chinese market due to GI registrations.

In another welcome development, in July 2014 at the S&ED, China committed to develop regulatory amendments to assert better regulatory control over manufacturers of bulk chemicals that can be used as active pharmaceutical ingredients in counterfeit drugs. China recognized the goal of fighting against the illegal manufacture, distribution, and export of counterfeit and substandard pharmaceutical products. In the June 2015 meeting of the S&ED, China further agreed to publish revisions to the Drug Administration Law in draft form for public comment and to take into account the opinions of the United States and other relevant stakeholders. The United States will continue to work with China to ensure that it fulfills its commitments in this important area.

Patent-Related Measures and Policies

IPR and Technological Standards

The growing importance of IPR and technological standards in China heightens U.S. concerns regarding a range of Chinese government policies and practices. Whereas open, voluntary, and consensus based standards best promote economic development, efficiency and innovation, standards development bodies in China have reportedly often denied membership or participation rights to foreign parties based on opaque and exclusionary practices, and effectively prevented foreign parties from participating in the standards setting process. In addition to the problem of excluding foreign firms from standards setting, there is also the concern that patent holders may be forced to contribute proprietary technologies to standards (and to license them to implementers) against their will, based on a number of provisions found in existing and proposed measures pertaining to technical regulations, standard essential patents, and Anti Monopoly Law enforcement. It is critical that China ensure that a patent holder's determination of whether to contribute technology to a standard and to make attendant licensing commitments are voluntary and without government intervention.

To address these concerns in part, the United States secured commitments in the 2015 JCCT where China stated that it welcomes U.S. invested firms in China to participate in the development of national recommendatory and social organization standards in China on a non discriminatory basis and that licensing commitments for patents in voluntary standards should be made voluntarily and without government involvement in negotiations over such commitments, except as otherwise provided by legally binding measures. These commitments represent progress and

[4] OECD, Trade in Counterfeit and Pirated Goods: Mapping the Economic Impact, http://www.oecd.org/gov/risk/trade-in-counterfeit-and-pirated-goods-9789264252653-en.htm

are welcome, but China will need to definitively address, including through the standards reform process that was set in motion in 2015, concerns that foreign entities are being excluded from standard setting processes, as well as concerns that patent holders and other participants are involuntarily forced to contribute technology to standards or license on certain terms.

Anti-monopoly Law (AML) Enforcement

Based on a limited number of investigations conducted to date, there is ongoing concern among U.S. companies that Chinese competition authorities may target for investigation those foreign firms that hold IPR that may be essential to the implementation of certain technological standards. Reports of intimidating and non-transparent investigative conduct contribute to these concerns. To promote improvements in AML enforcement policy, the United States has secured a number of commitments from China at the 2014 and 2015 meetings of the S&ED and JCCT. In addition to important commitments on procedural fairness and transparency, and access to counsel, China confirmed that the objective of competition policy is to promote consumer welfare and economic efficiency rather than promote individual competitors or industries; that enforcement of competition laws should be fair, objective, transparent, and non-discriminatory; and that China's AML enforcement agencies are to be free from intervention from other agencies in enforcement proceedings. China also committed that, taking into account the pro-competitive effects of intellectual property licensing, it attaches great importance to maintaining coherence in the rules related to IPR in the context of the AML.

IPR Protection for Pharmaceutical Innovations

The United States has engaged intensively with China to address obstacles to obtaining and maintaining patents on pharmaceutical innovations. Although the State Intellectual Property Office guidelines governing the review of patent applications were once generally consistent with those of the United States and leading patent offices in other countries, a subsequent revised interpretation of the guidelines severely restricted a patent applicant's ability to provide supplemental data in support of an application. As a result, China has, in some cases, denied pharmaceutical patent applications and invalidated existing patents, while the United States and other jurisdictions have generally granted patent protection in similar cases.

China's departure from its prior practice and that of other major patent offices was the subject of great attention during Vice President Biden's visit to Beijing in November 2013 and the annual meeting of the JCCT the following month. These engagements resulted in China's revision of its policy on data supplementation in late 2013, and a commitment to work with the United States to follow up on implementation, including the examination of individual cases. However, industry generally reports only partial progress as a result of the change, and that continued unjustified denials of patent applications and invalidations of existing patents create great uncertainty and potentially undermine incentives to innovate, including for China's nascent pharmaceutical innovators.

The United States continues to have concerns about the extent to which China provides effective protection against unfair commercial use of, as well as unauthorized disclosure of, and reliance on, undisclosed test or other data generated to obtain marketing approval for pharmaceutical products. China has undertaken commitments to ensure that no subsequent applicant may rely on the undisclosed test or other data submitted in support of an application for marketing approval of new pharmaceutical products for a period of at least six years from the date of marketing approval in China. However, there are reports that generic manufacturers have, in fact, been granted marketing approvals by the China Food and Drug Administration (CFDA) prior to the expiration of this period, and in some cases, even before the originator's product has been approved.

The United States was encouraged by China's 2012 JCCT commitment to define "new chemical entity," a term that is central to the application of data protection in the marketing approval process, in a manner consistent with international R&D practice. However, on March 4, 2016, China put into effect a Work Plan for the Reform of Chemical Drug Registration Categories, which limits the definition of "new drugs" to only those drugs for which marketing approval is first sought in China. This approach is inconsistent with the harmonized practice of the International Council for Harmonisation of Technical Requirements for Pharmaceuticals for Human Use. The lack of effective implementation of its 2012 JCCT commitment is a continued concern that China should address.

The United States has engaged closely with China to increase efficiency in regulatory approval processes for pharmaceuticals and medical devices to accelerate patient access and incentives to innovate and market new products in China. The United States welcomed China's commitment at the 2014 JCCT to reform its authorization processes and to add personnel and funding. However, some proposals related to the implementation of these reforms have raised serious concerns. For instance, the proposals appear to contain provisions that would provide regulatory incentives for companies to shift manufacturing capacity to China or participate in selected national projects and programs. Proposals such as these may have lasting negative effects on promoting global innovation and would appear more consistent with forced technology transfer industrial policies. The United States urges China to consider its current approach and adopt rules and procedures that are aligned with international best practices.

The United States looks forward to continuing to work with China to resolve these and other issues.

INDONESIA

Indonesia remains on the Priority Watch List in 2016. The United States welcomes Indonesia's recent focus on IPR. In particular, the United States recognizes positive steps that Indonesia has taken in the area of copyright protection, such as continued implementation of copyright reforms that were passed in 2014 and the establishment of a Creative Economy Agency. The United States is encouraged by Indonesia's announcement of reforms to its restrictive negative investment list for a number of intellectual property intensive sectors. The United States also applauds continued educational outreach to the Indonesian public to advance IPR awareness. Nevertheless, the United States remains concerned about gaps in Indonesia's laws relating to the protection and enforcement of IPR and urges Indonesia to address these issues.

The United States is concerned about widespread piracy and counterfeiting in Indonesia, particularly with respect to the lack of enforcement against dangerous products. It is essential that Indonesia fully fund and support a robust IPR enforcement effort. The United States encourages Indonesia to address this problem through greater coordination between the National Inter Ministerial IPR Task Force and Creative Economy Agency, as well as to create a specialized IPR unit under the Indonesia National Police (INP) that would focus on investigating the Indonesian criminal syndicates behind counterfeiting and piracy, and that would initiate larger and more significant cases. Enforcement cooperation among relevant agencies is essential, including with the

Directorate General for Intellectual Property (DGIP) and Badan Pengawas Obat dan Makanan, the regulatory agency that focuses on fake and substandard food and drug products. Further, the United States suggests increased coordination between the INP and the Attorney General's Office so that specialized IPR inspectors and prosecutors can enhance the effectiveness and efficiency of their investigations. Finally, the United States encourages deterrent level penalties for IPR infringement in physical markets and over the Internet.

The United States continues to encourage Indonesia to provide an effective system for protecting against the unfair commercial use, as well as unauthorized disclosure, of undisclosed test or other data generated to obtain marketing approval for pharmaceutical and agricultural chemical products. The United States also remains concerned about market access barriers in Indonesia, including measures related to the importation of motion pictures and measures that appear to condition permissions to import medicines on at least some local manufacturing or technology transfer requirements. As Indonesia considers amendments to its patent law, the United States urges Indonesia to provide interested stakeholders with meaningful opportunities to provide input. The United States also remains concerned about the lack of clarity surrounding legal procedures under the Indonesian patent law in connection with the grant of compulsory licenses. The United States encourages Indonesia to provide for judicial or other independent review of any compulsory license authorizations. The United States welcomes increased engagement with the Government of Indonesia, including through the IPR Working Group of the United States-Indonesia Trade and Investment Framework, to work toward substantively resolving these important issues.

THAILAND

Thailand remains on the Priority Watch List in 2016. The United States welcomes Thailand's stated desire to improve IPR protection and enforcement, including recent remarks by the Prime Minister acknowledging the importance of respecting IPR and the role IPR plays in making the Thai economy competitive. At the same time, IPR enforcement does not seem to be a top priority for Thai law enforcement, and there has been limited improvement of poor coordination among government entities despite the launch of the National IP Center of Enforcement in 2013. The United States urges Thailand to do more to prioritize IPR enforcement and to address longstanding organizational challenges. The Thai government took several legislative steps in 2014, including an amendment to the Customs Act that provides Thai customs officers with *ex officio* authority to suspend and seize illegal goods in transit, as well as copyright law amendments to address unauthorized camcording. Unfortunately, the Thai government in drafting several of the Copyright Act amendments failed to give weight to concerns expressed by foreign governments and industry on prior drafts of the law, such as omitting a much needed landlord liability provision. As a result, the amendments do not provide adequate protections against the circumvention of TPMs and the unauthorized modification of rights management information, nor do the amendments address procedural obstacles to enforcement against unauthorized camcording. Another Copyright Act amendment, introducing an option for right holders to obtain a court order to force online service providers to take down infringing content, has resulted in a lack of clarity in the operation of the notice and takedown procedures. Right holders also express concerns regarding pending legislation imposing content quota restrictions and the unintended effects of data and cyber security laws. It will be critical for Thai authorities to engage closely with foreign governments and industry as this and other legislation take shape. Other concerns include a backlog in pending patent applications, widespread use of unlicensed software in both the public and private sectors, growing Internet based copyright piracy, rampant trademark counterfeiting, lengthy civil IPR proceedings and low civil damages, and extensive cable and satellite signal theft. The United States continues to encourage Thailand to provide an effective system for protecting against the unfair commercial use, as well as unauthorized disclosure, of undisclosed test or other data generated to obtain marketing approval for pharmaceutical and agricultural chemical products. The United States urges Thailand to engage in a meaningful and transparent manner with all relevant stakeholders, including IPR owners, as it considers ways to address Thailand's public health challenges, while maintaining a patent system that promotes innovation. The United States looks forward to continuing to work with Thailand to address these and other issues.

SOUTH AND CENTRAL ASIA

INDIA

India remains on the Priority Watch List in 2016. Since the conclusion of an OCR focused on bilateral engagement in 2014, India has maintained strong channels of engagement with the United States on IPR issues, improved communication with industry stakeholders, increasingly publicly recognized the importance of IPR and linked it to India's future development, and taken positive steps to address or avoid further erosions of the IPR regime. India's courts retain their reputation for providing fair and deliberate treatment of both foreign and domestic litigants. However, at the same time, India has not taken the opportunity to address long standing and systemic deficiencies in its IPR regime and has endorsed problematic policies that may leave open the door for backsliding in the future. In 2016, the United States continues to prioritize making progress on IPR issues through the High Level Working Group on Intellectual Property (IP Working Group), established by President Obama and Prime Minister Modi. In this bilateral dialogue, the United States is working with India to foster an environment that will enable India to achieve its important domestic policy goals of increasing investment and stimulating innovation through, not at the expense of, IPR protection and enforcement. Attention to our IPR priorities and action to resolve concerns through bilateral fora can benefit both the United States and India. The IP Working Group will continue to prioritize substantive and measurable action.

The United States has welcomed efforts undertaken by the Modi Administration to promote IPR within India and the steps it has taken to strengthen protection and enforcement. High level national initiatives, such as "Make in India" and "Start up India" have linked the realization of development goals to IPR creation and protection. The 2015 passage of the Commercial Courts, Commercial Division and Commercial Appellate Division of High Courts Bill may provide an important new tool for right holders in India to efficiently and effectively enforce their rights in the courts. The hiring and training of large numbers of new patent and trademark examiners should help to reduce significant delays new applicants face while also cutting down the backlog of pending applications. Significant state level enforcement developments included the establishment of India's first anti piracy policy unit in Telangana and Andhra Pradesh's anti piracy campaign, which resulted in the arrest of 11 individuals involved in an international piracy ring. The United States also welcomed the deliberate and transparent process employed in India's evaluation of a compulsory license application in 2015.

In other areas, however, recent actions have raised new concerns. For example, India's proposed Patent Rule Amendments would introduce concerning new incentives to pressure patent applicants to localize manufacturing in India and require the submission of sensitive business information to India's Patent Office. The unpredictable application of Section 3(d) of the Patents Act has led to additional rejections of patent applications for innovative pharmaceutical products. In addition, India has also introduced unpredictability for patent applicants through the issuance of guidelines on the patentability of computer related inventions following an opaque process for soliciting comments.

India has also not taken the opportunity to address longstanding challenges that represent significant IPR regime deficiencies compared to other markets. The pharmaceutical industry in particular faces a host of challenges related to IPR. These include irregularities in the application of Section 3(d) of India's Patents Act; the lack of an effective system for protecting against unfair commercial use, as well as the unauthorized disclosure, of undisclosed test or other data generated to obtain marketing approval for pharmaceutical products; lack of clarity on standards for Sections 85 and 92 compulsory licenses and revocation under Section 66; and the lack of an effective system for notifying interested parties of marketing approvals for generic pharmaceuticals in a manner that would allow for the early resolution of potential patent disputes. For industries that create and supply content, high levels of piracy and unpredictability in the market undermine a vibrant and competitive sector for Indian and U.S. companies. Brand owners also face delays and challenges in obtaining trademarks, and rampant counterfeit products in the market. India has yet to develop legislation that would ensure trade secrets are adequately protected against misappropriation. Further, India has not yet joined important international IPR treaties, such as the WCT, the WPPT, and the Singapore Treaty.

These concerns are subjects of our revitalized dialogue within the IP Working Group and will continue to be prioritized. The United States is hopeful that, as India's policymakers increasingly view the creation of IPR as valuable and supportive of an innovative economy that can keep pace with global trade developments, progress on these and other issues is possible. The United States remains committed to the work being conducted under the IP Working Group, including hosting the Indian Government for a Copyright Workshop in April 2016 and participating in a Trade Secrets Workshop in India later in 2016.

National IPR Policy

The Government of India is in the final stages of its thorough and holistic review of the IPR regime to "nurture the IP culture and address all facets of the IP system including legal, administrative and enforcement infrastructure, human resources, institutional support system and international dimensions." A body of government selected experts (known as the IPR Think Tank) produced the first draft of the National IPR Policy[5] for public comment in December 2014. The United States submitted comments to the Government of India on this draft in January 2015 and has maintained an active dialogue on this issue since that time. The United States has commended India for undertaking this task, noting, in particular, the mutual interests both countries have in areas identified by the IPR Think Tank as target issues for Indian policymakers: transparency and stakeholder consultation; coordination among national and state authorities; public awareness; legal and legislative reforms; administration; commercialization; and enforcement. While the United States understands that the Government of India is approaching the release of the official version of the National IPR Policy, the United States continues to urge India to allow interested

[5] India's Draft National IPR Policy, December 19, 2014, available at: http://dipp.nic.in/English/Schemes/Intellectual_Property_Rights/IPR_Policy_24December2014.pdf

parties to review and provide comments that would help strengthen the document and provide clarity to assist the implementing authorities to effect substantive changes in India's IPR regime. A lackluster policy that does not reflect or provide the ability to act upon Prime Minister Modi and high level officials' stated commitment to improve the climate for IPR in India would be an unfortunate missed opportunity.

Copyright and Piracy

The United States continues to seek changes to India's copyright protection and enforcement regime that would protect both Indian and U.S. right holders in the vibrant and promising Indian market. In particular, the United States urges India to: enact anti camcording legislation; model its statutory license provisions relating to copyrighted works on the standards of the Berne Convention for the Protection of Literary and Artistic Works (Berne Convention); ensure that collecting societies are licensed promptly and able to operate effectively; fully establish and operationalize India's Copyright Boards; address the problem of underreporting of cable subscriptions; take steps to prevent India's public broadcasters from facilitating the dissemination of pirated content; and provide additional protections against signal theft, circumvention of TPMs, and online copyright piracy. At the same time, additional resources should be devoted to develop more effective enforcement strategies. This is an area of substantial common interest between the United States and India, as both countries have vibrant content producers and distribution channels.

The United States and India announced important developments with respect to copyright through the 2015 Trade Policy Forum (TPF) Joint Statement. Both countries "agreed to deepen cooperation on copyright, recognizing the shared interest of the largest entertainment industries in the world to promote and protect their artistic and creative content." As part of this effort, the United States hosted a delegation of Indian government officials involved in copyright protection and enforcement, as well as U.S. and industry stakeholders, for a two day workshop in April 2016. Through this effort, a clearer picture emerged of the challenges facing right holders and the tools that could effectively curb piracy and promote content creation. The cost of piracy is already massive industry reports that losses from piracy of music and movies in India are approximately $4 billion per year and the commercial value of unlicensed software approaches $3 billion. At the same time, the opportunities in India are massive and growing in India's $17 billion media and entertainment industry. India's outlets to bring content to consumers are flourishing, with a growing number of innovative digital platforms, over 800 television channels, 139 million pay TV households, and 94,000 newspapers. This trend makes it all the more imperative that India incorporate into its legal system more effective measures to counter online piracy. The United States encourages the Government of India to adopt effective measures to counter online piracy, including appropriate notice and takedown procedures and other efficient mechanisms for right holders to seek removal of infringing content from websites, consistent with international best practices. The United States also encourages the Government of India to undertake a review of its applicable statutory damages provisions for copyright piracy to ensure that they are appropriately calibrated to have a deterrent effect.

The high incidence of camcording in India underscores the importance of developing an effective legal framework to address this problem. India has one of the highest rates of video piracy in the world, according to a 2013 study conducted by the Motion Pictures Distributors Association of India. This study found that incidents originating in India accounted for approximately half of all such incidents in the Asia Pacific region in that year. The 2015 TPF Joint Statement included a call to action to address our shared "concern about the unauthorized recording, including camcording, of films in cinemas and copyright piracy on websites." While the United

States welcomed India's commitment to "positive reforms relating to anti camcording measures proposed in forthcoming amendments to the existing Indian Cinematograph Act in the draft Cinematographic Bill," these amendments have not yet been considered by the Indian Parliament.

The United States encourages India to take additional steps to improve coordination with enforcement officials of Indian state governments. As noted above, right holders and the United States commend the Andhra Pradesh anti piracy cell's actions against an international piracy ring which resulted in 11 arrests. The establishment of the Telangana Intellectual Property Crime Unit in December 2015, which brings together officials from the cyber crime police, IT ministry, ISPs, film industry, and legal and financial experts, holds promise for creating new effective solutions to combat piracy. If successful, this strategy could provide a model for anti piracy efforts nationwide.

To strengthen engagement on these and other copyright issues, and to build upon the strengths of the vibrant Indian and U.S. copyright intensive industries, including in movies, music, and software, the United States welcomes closer bilateral cooperation with India and hopes that the successful 2016 Copyright Workshop may be continued and expanded upon in the future.

Patents & Regulatory Data Protection

The United States continues to encourage India to promote an efficient, transparent, and predictable patent system that nurtures and incentivizes innovation. As leading economies with strong traditions of innovation, India and the United States can and should ensure supportive, enabling environments for innovators at all stages of the innovation lifecycle to achieve success and contribute significantly to economic growth. The United States commends India on actions taken in recent years to improve the operations of its Patent Office, such as digitizing records, upgrading online search and e filing capabilities, and hiring additional patent examiners. India announced plans to hire and train an additional 459 patent examiners in 2016 which should help reduce pendency. India's demonstrated commitment to address these issues will help promote efficiency, transparency, and predictability in patent administration in India, to the benefit of domestic and foreign innovators, and to India overall.

With respect to patents, the United States continues to have serious concerns about the innovation climate for a number of sectors, including biopharmaceuticals, agricultural chemicals, software, and green technology. Innovators in these sectors face serious challenges in securing and enforcing patents in India. This is not only detrimental to these commercial interests, but also impedes economic growth in India, as it discourages companies from entering the Indian market or engaging in the kinds of voluntary and mutually agreed technology development and transfer that India is seeking domestically and in multilateral fora. In fact, India has rejected patents that were granted in many other jurisdictions, including the United States. The United States urges India to reject policies and practices that amount to barriers that adversely affect not only U.S. companies, but Indian companies as well. The United States encourages India instead to adopt policies that both address domestic challenges and support the cutting edge innovation that can be critical to meeting legitimate domestic policy goals.

For example, a patent system should encourage the development of inventions that meet the well established international criteria, enshrined in the TRIPS Agreement, of being new, involving an inventive step, and being capable of industrial application. Consistent with this, Section 2(j) of India's Patents Act sets forth the criteria for patentability. An "invention" under the Act is any product or process that is novel, has an inventive step, and is capable of industrial application. However, Section 3(d) of India's Patents Act states, in relevant part, that "the mere discovery of a new form of a known substance which does not result in the enhancement of the known efficacy of that substance" is not considered to be an "invention" under Indian law.[6]

The United States continues to have concerns that Section 3(d) of India's Patents Act, as interpreted, may have the effect of limiting the patentability of potentially beneficial innovations. Such innovations could include drugs with fewer side effects, decreased toxicity, improved delivery systems, or temperature or storage stability. In practice, India has already applied this standard to deny patent protection to potentially beneficial innovations, some of which enjoy patent protection in many other jurisdictions. Furthermore, the unpredictable application of Section 3(d) creates considerable uncertainty for patent applicants and patent holders. This uncertainty is exacerbated by the ability of third parties to use Section 3(d) as the basis for challenging patents, either before or after they are granted, which can potentially lead to revocation or delays that result in an extremely costly reduction in patent term that cannot be recouped. Section 3(d)'s negative effects are not borne entirely by foreign companies. In fact, Indian firms that have received patents in the United States and other jurisdictions have been denied patents by India. India should reconsider Section 3(d) in light of its domestic priorities of promoting innovation, improving ease of doing business, and strengthening IPR systems. In the immediate term, clarifying the application of the current law would help ensure patent applications are not denied for innovative products which build upon existing technology.

In addition, the United States supports patent systems that incorporate efficient patent procedures and foster high quality patents; as such, the United States urges India to improve and streamline its patent opposition procedures. Specifically, under India's patent regime, the same interested party may, at minimal cost, challenge a patent through both pre grant and post grant opposition proceedings on any of 11 enumerated grounds, including by citing the same grounds in both pre and post grant challenges. As a result, applications can be tied up in costly challenge proceedings for years, all the while running the potential term of the patent, which begins from the application filing date. This limits an applicant's ability to make investments and conduct business in India.

Reexamining policies that impose significant burdens on patent applicants and India's already severely taxed patent office would help to further reduce the patent application backlog and encourage additional investment in India. The Patents Act's requirements under Section 8 are out of step with the practices of other countries and out of date, as much of the information required is readily available to patent officers online. Furthermore, "Form 27" requires patent holders to provide detailed information on an annual basis that is used by the patent office to determine whether a patent is sufficiently worked in India. Patentees thus face the serious consequence of possibly having their patent revoked or subject to a compulsory license if they fail to meet the standard. While the United States welcomes the Indian Patent Office's efforts in recent years to publish patent examination guidelines, e.g., in the pharmaceutical and software fields, there remain significant areas of uncertainty. With respect to the computer related invention guidelines, there was a lack of transparency in the process used to arrive at the current set of guidelines and the guidelines reflect a seemingly narrow interpretation of the relevant law, both of which raise concerns and threaten to undermine an important sector of India's economy.

The United States welcomes India's efforts to address the significant patent pendency (reported to run three to five years) and backlog situation, including through the hiring of new patent examiners. However, other methods India is exploring raise serious concerns and may ultimately undermine India's innovation and economic aspirations. In October 2015, India's Ministry of

---

[6] Section 3(d) contains a further Explanation stating that "[f]or the purposes of this clause [3(d)], salts, esters, ethers, polymorphs, metabolites, pure form, particle size, isomers, mixtures of isomers, complexes, combinations and other derivatives of known substance shall be considered to be the same substance, unless they differ significantly in properties with regard to efficacy."

Commerce and Industry issued The Patents (Amendment), Rules, 2015 (Patent Rule Amendments) in an effort to address this issue and reduce delays. Unfortunately, the proposal seeks to accomplish this by offering expedited patent examination for applicants that manufacture or commit to manufacture their inventions in India. This incentive to localize manufacturing goes against international patent norms and runs counter to increasingly globalized trade and sourcing trends.

While emphasizing our continued commitment to the Doha Declaration on the TRIPS Agreement and Public Health, (see **Intellectual Property and Health**), the United States also continues to monitor India's application of its compulsory licensing law. The United States requests clarity from the Government of India regarding the compulsory license decision making process, as it affects U.S. stakeholders. In particular, the United States requests further clarification that could increase confidence for patentees such that they better understand the conditions for which a compulsory license would be permitted. Although the government has issued only one compulsory license under Section 84 of India's Patents Act and recently rejected another Section 84 petition, India has made clear in other policy statements that it views compulsory licensing as an important tool of industrial policy for green technologies, with the potential to be applied more regularly across economic sectors. Specifically, India has, in the past, promoted compulsory licensing in its National Manufacturing Policy as a mechanism available for government entities to effectuate technology transfer in the clean energy sector. More recently, an April 2015 draft of what the media reported to be an updated copy of the National IPR Policy included a call for "the acquisition of environment friendly technologies through voluntary and involuntary licensing, creation of patent pools, technology transfer, and other business collaboration arrangements."

The United States also notes with concern the continuing challenges involved with the enforcement of patent rights in India, including difficulties that some patent holders reportedly face in securing injunctions against firms that manufacture patented inventions without authorization from the patent holder. In addition, Indian state governmental authorities reportedly do not have a mechanism to confirm whether an item to be manufactured and for which marketing approval is sought is under patent. While patent holders have successfully upheld their rights in some recent court cases, the cost of litigation and significant delays erode the value of a patent, underscoring the need for greater transparency and regulatory coordination between officials in state and central governments.

Finally, the United States continues to urge India to provide an effective system for protecting against unfair commercial use, as well as the unauthorized disclosure, of undisclosed test or other data generated to obtain marketing approval for pharmaceutical and agricultural chemical products. Without these types of protections, companies in India reportedly are able to copy certain pharmaceutical products and seek immediate government approval for marketing based on the original developer's data. The United States notes the statement from the IPR Think Tank in its draft National IPR Policy that describes protection of undisclosed information as an "important area of study and research for future policy development."

Trade Secrets

The United States continues to note its concern regarding trade secret protection in India, particularly the reported difficulty in obtaining remedies and damages. India appears to rely primarily upon contract and common law to provide trade secret protection. Although India's approach may address the theft of trade secrets where a contract has been breached, it appears to be less effective in covering situations in which there is no contractual relationship, such as in cases of theft by a business competitor. Although Indian law does provide for some remedies, including injunctive relief, in practice, damages can be very difficult to obtain. Finally, because India's court system reportedly lacks sufficient procedural safeguards to protect trade secrets or other confidential information divulged through discovery in civil or criminal litigation, there is a risk that such information may be disclosed publicly in the course of judicial proceedings, deterring victims of trade secret theft from using the court system to enforce their rights. The United States notes positive statements in the first draft of India's National IPR Policy that seek to address gaps in the legal framework with respect to adequately protecting trade secrets in India. The United States also welcomed India's announcement in the 2015 TPF joint statement that India is committed "to strong protection of trade secrets." The United States looks forward to the opportunity to discuss this issue under the IP Working Group and share new legislative approaches, including through holding a joint workshop in 2016.

Trademarks and Counterfeiting

The United States continues to receive stakeholder concerns regarding burdensome procedures for acquiring a trademark and significant delays associated with cancellation and opposition proceedings at the administrative level of the Trademark Registry. While industry reports progress on police, customs, and judicial enforcement, resources currently devoted to these institutions are insufficient given the scope of the problem and right holders report significant delays.

In addition, the level of production, sale, distribution, importation, and exportation of counterfeit goods affecting India's market remains very troubling. (See Border and Criminal Enforcement Against Counterfeiting). The first draft of India's National IPR Policy notes that the Government of India should have an interest in strongly combating copyright piracy and trademark counterfeiting, as these illicit activities harm consumers and legitimate producers in India. As described in Border and Criminal Enforcement Against Counterfeiting, U.S. consumers may be harmed by fraudulent and potentially dangerous counterfeit products, particularly medicines, originating in India. Producers face the risk of diminished profits and loss of reputation when consumers purchase fake products, and governments lose tax revenue and find it more difficult to attract investment. Infringers generally pay no taxes or duties and often disregard basic standards for worker health and safety and product quality and performance.

U.S. enforcement authorities continue to express concerns about counterfeit and pirated goods produced in India and shipped to the United States. Some of these products (e.g., counterfeit pharmaceuticals) pose serious risks to U.S. consumers. The United States welcomes opportunities for enhanced bilateral engagement with India on IPR related border enforcement issues. Such cooperation could include sharing best practices, customs to customs information exchange for use in risk management and enforcement actions, and conducting joint customs enforcement operations designed to deter and interdict shipments of IPR infringing goods destined for the United States.

Localization Trends

The United States remains concerned about actions and policies in India that appear to favor local manufacturing or Indian IPR owners in a manner that distorts the competitive landscape needed to ensure the development of globally successful and innovative industries. For example, under India's Drug Price Control Order, the National Pharmaceutical Pricing Authority implemented pricing restrictions on 509 drug formulations, effective April 1, 2015. However, exemptions from those restrictions allow certain medicines that are manufactured in India and "developed using indigenous R&D," to be priced higher, providing an advantage to Indian companies. India also increased or reinstated customs duties in 2016 on a broad range of innovative and IP intensive goods, including medical devices, lifesaving drugs, information and communications technology products, solar energy equipment, and capital goods, citing that the duties were intended to promote local manufacturing. In 2016, India also announced wide sweeping duty increases on information and communications technology, electronics, capital goods, medical devices and clean energy goods, while at the same time removing duty exemptions on pharmaceuticals and defense equipment. According to government statements, the duty increases are intended to boost manufacturing in India, apparently through the use of import substitution. In addition, the Indian Intellectual Property Appellate Board's interpretation of Section 84 of India's Patents Act suggests that a patent could be subject to a compulsory license if the patented product is not manufactured in India. Further, despite a Central Drug Standard Control Organization Office Order on waiver of local clinical trial requirements, industry still faces inconsistent application of requirements for local clinical trial data for approval of new drugs. In the information and communications technology sector, U.S. industry cites in country testing requirements and data and server localization requirements as inhibiting market access in India. Further, as described in detail above, India's proposed Patent Rule Amendments, if enacted, would impose concerning new measures that appear designed to pressure companies to localize their manufacturing to India.

While the United States welcomes the steps that India has taken over the past year to recognize the positive impact of IPR on India's development, improve the administration of India's IPR regime, and take affirmative steps on certain IPR challenges, such as enforcement and the establishment of new courts, deeper and more comprehensive action is necessary to address the serious deficiencies that remain. The United States looks forward to continuing to work with the Government of India to prioritize this work while responding to new challenges.

NEAR EAST, INCLUDING NORTH AFRICA

ALGERIA

Algeria remains on the Priority Watch List in 2016. The United States commends Algeria for acceding to the Madrid Protocol in 2015 and for its ongoing effort to promote awareness of the importance of IPR in Algeria. The United States notes, however, that despite these actions, much more remains to be done in the area of IPR enforcement, particularly, enforcement of existing anti piracy statutes, including combating the use of unlicensed software, and the provision of judicial remedies in the event of patent infringement. The United States encourages Algeria to provide an effective system for protecting against unfair commercial use, as well as unauthorized disclosure, of undisclosed test or other data generated to obtain marketing approval for pharmaceutical products. Algeria's ban on an increased number of imported pharmaceutical products and medical devices in favor of local products is a trade matter of utmost concern and the primary reason that Algeria remains on the Priority Watch List. The United States urges Algeria to remove this market access barrier, and looks forward to continuing its engagement with Algeria, including in the context of Algeria's efforts to accede to the WTO.

KUWAIT

Kuwait remains on the Priority Watch List in 2016. Kuwait was elevated from the Watch List in November 2014 at the conclusion of an OCR, because Kuwait failed to introduce to the National Assembly a copyright law consistent with international standards, and had not resumed effective enforcement against copyright and trademark infringement. Although Kuwaiti officials initially took steps to resume enforcement following the announcement of the 2014 OCR, effective enforcement actions have reportedly significantly decreased since June 2015, particularly against trade in counterfeit goods. The United States awaits improvements in copyright and trademark enforcement and the passage of long overdue copyright legislation that is consistent with Kuwait's international commitments. The United States stands ready to work with Kuwait toward resolving these important issues.

EUROPE AND EURASIA

RUSSIA

Russia remains on the Priority Watch List in 2016 as a result of continued and significant challenges to IPR protection and enforcement, particularly in the areas of copyright infringement, trademark counterfeiting (with a notable increase in counterfeit branded seeds) and non transparent collecting society procedures. In particular, the United States remains concerned over stakeholder reports that IPR enforcement continued to decline overall in 2015, following similar declines in the prior three years including a reduction in resources for enforcement personnel. There are also reports that IPR is not a priority for government officials.

Copyright infringement is a persistent problem in Russia, including, but not limited to, online piracy. Although Russia's antipiracy legislation continues to evolve, its efficacy and the possible need for further modifications remain uncertain. In one positive development, a Russian court shut down Rutracker.org, which had been listed in the Notorious Markets List. However, Russia remains home to many other sites (such as vKontakte) that facilitate online piracy, damaging both the market for legitimate content in Russia as well as in other countries. Issuing injunctions against infringing websites does not address the root of the problem; Russia should be investigating and prosecuting the operators of such sites. The overall number of raids, criminal charges, and convictions have declined in recent years. The United States urges Russia to ensure that ongoing legislative and enforcement efforts will result in copyright enforcement mechanisms that are fair, effective, and transparent.

The lack of enforcement of trademarks has resulted in the continued problem of counterfeit goods in Russia. Stakeholders express concern that counterfeit goods continue to be manufactured, transshipped and sold in Russia, including counterfeit seeds, agricultural chemicals, electronics, information technology, auto parts, consumer goods, machinery, and other products. The Russian Ministry of Agriculture estimated in 2015 that 10 to 20 percent of hybrid sunflower, rapeseed, and soybean seed used in Russia was counterfeit. The smuggling of Chinese origin counterfeit products continued through Kazakhstan and the Kyrgyz Republic into Russia. While the United States applauds Russia's development of an officially approved methodology for testing allegedly counterfeit pharmaceuticals, counterfeit pharmaceuticals continue to be manufac tured in Russia and made available through online pharmacies.

The United States is also concerned about Russia's implementation of the commitments it made in the WTO Working Party Report related to the protection against unauthorized disclosure of, or reliance on, undisclosed test or other data generated to obtain marketing approval for pharmaceutical products. Although Russia amended its Law on Circulation of Medicines, it has not issued the final regulations that include the detailed provisions necessary to ensure the implementation of such protection.

The United States urges Russia to develop a more comprehensive, transparent and effective legal framework and enforcement strategy to reduce IPR infringement, particularly the sale of counterfeit goods, and the piracy of copyright protected content. Although the United States has curtailed bilateral engagement with Russia on a myriad of issues in response to Russia's actions in Ukraine, the United States continues to monitor Russia's progress on these and other matters through appropriate channels.

UKRAINE

Ukraine remains on the Priority Watch List in 2016. Ukraine was designated a Priority Foreign Country (PFC) in the 2013 Special 301 Report. As described in that report, the three grounds for Ukraine's PFC designation were: (1) the unfair, nontransparent administration of the system for collecting societies, which are responsible for collecting and distributing royalties to U.S. and other right holders; (2) widespread (and admitted) use of unlicensed software by Ukrainian government agencies; and (3) failure to implement an effective means to combat the widespread online infringement of copyright and related rights in Ukraine, including the lack of transparent and predictable provisions on intermediary liability and liability for third parties that facilitate piracy, limitations on such liability for ISPs and enforcement of takedown notices for infringing online content.

The United States recognizes that Ukraine has taken some positive steps under extremely trying circumstances. A special unit was created within the National Police of Ukraine to investigate IPR violations and enforcement officials have participated in international trainings on investigating IPR crimes. More broadly, the government appears to be working to address long standing concerns about endemic corruption and mismanagement, including in IPR protection and enforcement. However, evidence of real progress is still not apparent and enforcement remains inadequate.

The United States is looking for more progress in addressing the three problems identified in the *2013 Special 301 Report*. With respect to unauthorized collecting societies, little has changed. In the past year, the government has de credited one of the "rogue" collecting societies and reportedly suspended two more societies pending investigation. However, approximately 15 other collecting societies continue to operate, collecting royalties without paying right holders. Moreover, efforts to pass legislation to address the underlying legal deficiencies of the collecting society system in Ukraine have not progressed.

With respect to improving the government's response to online infringement, several attempts at legislative reform appear to have stalled. As highlighted in the 2015 Notorious Markets List, Ukraine continues to host some of the largest pirate sites in the world serving IP infringing content to a global audience.

Ukraine has taken some preliminary steps to reduce the use of unlicensed software by Ukrain ian government agencies. For example, unlicensed software used by one of the pilot government agencies was reduced by more than 50 percent. Moreover, in addition to continuing to audit the software used by several government agencies, the Government of Ukraine, consistent with its goal of increased transparency, made the results of its inspections public, online. Notwithstanding these improvements, the overall piracy rate in the government remains unacceptably high, at 60-80 percent. The United States expects the Ukrainian government to set an example for its citizens and business community by legalizing the software used in its own operations, and requiring high levels of transparency in other IPR related operations, such as its management of royalty collecting societies.

The Government of Ukraine has stated that it seeks to improve these and other IPR related deficiencies to advance its own agenda for economic improvement, particularly in promoting foreign direct investment, ensuring that legitimate Ukrainian creators and innovators can build successful businesses, and fulfilling its IPR related obligations under the EU-Ukraine Association Agreement. The United States looks forward to the new government turning its attention to addressing these long-standing problems. Tangible progress in this area will demonstrate that Ukraine is a stable and attractive investment climate. The United States will continue to engage with the Government of Ukraine.

WESTERN HEMISPHERE

ARGENTINA

Argentina remains on the 2016 Priority Watch List, as it continues to present a number of long-standing and well-known deficiencies in IPR protection and enforcement, and has become an extremely challenging market for IPR intensive industries. However, the United States is hopeful that the recently elected government of President Mauricio Macri will engage more productively to improve the protection and enforcement of IPR in Argentina, thereby creating a more attractive environment for investment and innovation.

A major challenge in Argentina is the lack of effective IPR enforcement by the national government. Argentine police do not take *ex officio* actions, prosecutions can stall, cases may languish in excessive formalities, and, even when a criminal investigation reaches final judgment, infringers do not receive deterrent sentences. In terms of physical counterfeiting and piracy, the notorious market La Salada in Buenos Aires is one of the biggest open-air markets in Latin America offering counterfeit and pirated goods and it continues to grow. Efforts by the City of Buenos Aires in 2014 to combat increasing lawlessness in the market received little assistance from the national government and were unsuccessful. Recent warehouse raids and the Macri administration's public commitment to combat the growth of illegal street markets send a positive signal. While optical disc copyright piracy is widespread, Internet piracy is a growing concern. Internet piracy rates approach 100 percent in several content areas. For example, Argentine-run notorious market Cuevana – offering pirated movies and TV shows – expanded in 2015 to include a mobile streaming application. Criminal enforcement is nearly nonexistent. As a result, IPR enforcement in Argentina consists mainly of right holders trying to convince cooperative Argentine online providers to agree to take down specific infringing works, as well as attempting to seek injunctions in civil cases. Right holders also cite widespread use of unlicensed software by Argentine private enterprises and the government.

Finally, there are a number of ongoing challenges to innovation in the agricultural chemical, biotechnology, and pharmaceutical sectors, including with respect to patent pendency, scope and term of patent protection, and meaningful enforcement options. The United States remains concerned that Argentina does not appear to provide adequate protection against the unfair commercial use, as well as unauthorized disclosure, of undisclosed test or other data generated to obtain marketing approval for pharmaceutical or agricultural chemical products. Argentina only provides patent protection from the date of the grant of the patent and offers no provisional protection for pending patents. There is a substantial backlog of patent applications which results in long delays in registering rights. Argentina rejects patent applications with claims for common pharmaceutical products. To be patentable, Argentina requires that processes for the manufacture of active compounds disclosed in a specification be reproducible and applicable on an industrial scale. Industry also asserts that Resolution 283/2015, introduced in September 2015, limits the ability to patent biotechnological innovations based on living matter and natural substances, including biologics. These measures limit the ability of companies investing in Argentina to protect their IPR and appear inconsistent with international practice.

CHILE

Chile remains on the Priority Watch List in 2016. The United States recognizes steps Chile made in 2015 to reduce processing times for patents, to increase IP enforcement actions, and reduce the rate of unlicensed software use. For example, in January 2016, authorities in Chile took action against a piracy group responsible for releasing more than 80 unauthorized "camcorded" copies on at least ten different websites. However, the United States continues to have serious concerns regarding longstanding IPR issues under the United States Chile Free Trade Agreement. The United States continues to urge Chile to implement both protections against the unlawful circumvention of TPMs and protections for encrypted program carrying satellite signals. Chile also needs to ensure that effective administrative and judicial procedures, as well as deterrent remedies, are made available to right holders and satellite and cable service providers, including measures to address ongoing concerns with decoder boxes. The United States continues to urge Chile to join UPOV 91 and improve protection for plant varieties. The United States also urges Chile to implement an effective system for addressing patent issues expeditiously in connection with applications to market pharmaceutical products and to provide adequate protection against unfair commercial use, as well as unauthorized disclosure, of undisclosed test or other data generated to obtain marketing approval for pharmaceutical products. Finally, the United States urges Chile to amend its ISP liability regime to permit effective action against piracy over the Internet.

Under the TPP Agreement, which sets strong and balanced standards on IPR protection and enforcement (See Trans Pacific Partnership), Chile has committed to strengthen its IPR regime in these and other areas. The United States will work closely with Chile on TPP implementation, including through technical assistance. The United States will also continue to address IPR issues through bilateral engagement.

VENEZUELA

Venezuela remains on the Priority Watch List in 2016, as there were no apparent efforts to improve Venezuela's IPR system in 2015. Venezuela's formal withdrawal from the Andean Community and the reinstatement of its 1956 Industrial Property Law, in conjunction with provisions in Venezuela's 1999 constitution and international treaty obligations still in effect, has created legal ambiguity for IPR and impeded the registration of patents for pharmaceutical products. Venezuela's Autonomous Intellectual Property Service (SAPI) has not issued a new patent since 2007, and, as of May 2015, SAPI has substantially increased patent filing and maintenance fees. Brand owners report that SAPI regularly approves and publishes applications for trademarks that are similar or nearly identical to registered marks and that trademark opposition procedures are slow and ineffective. Venezuela also fails to provide an effective system for protecting against the unfair commercial use, as well as unauthorized disclosure, of undisclosed test or other data generated to obtain marketing approval for pharmaceutical products. While the Venezuelan customs service has made some successful counterfeit seizures over the past year, IPR enforcement in general remains insufficient to address widespread counterfeiting and piracy, including online. Prosecutions of IP crimes are rare, adjudication of cases is slow, and penalties are insufficient to deter counterfeiters. In the past year, infringing copies of movies found to be contributing to online piracy were traced back to unauthorized camcording in Venezuelan theaters. Consistent with this stagnant IPR picture, the Property Rights Alliance's 2015 Intellectual Property Rights Index ranked Venezuela 125 of the 129 countries evaluated, and the World Economic Forum's 2015 2016 Competitiveness Report ranked Venezuela last among all 140 countries evaluated with respect to IPR protection.

Watch List

EAST ASIA AND THE PACIFIC

VIETNAM

Vietnam remains on the Watch List in 2016. Online piracy and sales of counterfeit goods over the Internet continue to be common. As more Vietnamese obtain broadband Internet access and purchase smartphones, the United States expects that online piracy and sales of counterfeit goods will continue to worsen unless the Government of Vietnam takes significant action. Counterfeit goods including counterfeits of high quality also remain widely available in physical markets, and, while still limited, domestic manufacturing of counterfeit goods is emerging as an issue. In addition, book piracy, software piracy, and cable and satellite signal theft persist. Enforcement continues to be a challenge for Vietnam. Capacity constraints persist partially due to a lack of resources and IPR expertise. Vietnam continues to rely heavily on administrative enforcement actions, which have failed to deter widespread counterfeiting and piracy. The United States will closely monitor amendments to the Penal Code that will go into effect in July 2016, which will establish criminal liability for organizations and business owners with respect to cer tain IPR violations. Vietnam's system for protecting against the unfair commercial use, as well as unauthorized disclosure of undisclosed test or other data generated to obtain marketing approval for pharmaceutical products also needs clarifications. The Government of Vietnam is in the process of drafting or revising circulars in a number of IPR related areas, including with respect to interagency cooperation on enforcement issues. Additionally, various Vietnamese agencies continue to engage in public awareness campaigns. However, various other impediments to doing business, such as investment and distribution barriers, have complicated efforts by foreign companies to sell legitimate products in Vietnam's market.

Under the TPP Agreement, which sets strong and balanced standards on IPR protection and enforcement (See Trans Pacific Partnership), Vietnam has committed to strengthen its IPR regime in these and other areas. The United States will work closely with Vietnam on TPP implementation, including through technical assistance and other trade capacity building. We also will continue to address IPR issues through bilateral engagement.

SOUTH AND CENTRAL ASIA

PAKISTAN

USTR is moving Pakistan from the Priority Watch List to the Watch List in 2016 with an OCR due to the Government of Pakistan's significant efforts to implement key provisions of the Intellectual Property Organization of Pakistan (IPO Pakistan) Act of 2012 and the newfound determination with which Pakistan has approached IPR over the past 12 months. Highlights of Pakistan's recent efforts to address salient IPR challenges include establishing and appointing IP Tribunals at Islamabad, Karachi, and Lahore; establishing a timeline for the amendment of major IPR laws; imminent implementation of the Federal Board of Revenue's (FBR) IP Enforcement Rules; undertaking public awareness programs on IPR protection; and committing to continue regular, action oriented engagement with the United States and stakeholders. Pakistan's IP Tribunals possess the potential to provide expert and efficient means for right holders to enforce their IPR in Pakistan which has often been cited as a key area of difficulty in the past. The Lahore Tribunal is already fully functional, with Karachi and Islamabad scheduled to follow within three months. All three tribunals are set to have drafted IP Judicial Benchbooks within six months and Pakistan has committed to a judicial exchange with the United States this summer.

Pakistan has committed to a transparent process for amending key IPR legislation. Revisions to laws on copyright, trademark, and patents are scheduled to be finalized by the end of 2016, following consultation with interested stakeholders and the United States. Pakistan also completed its draft Plant Breeders Act which now stands before the National Assembly. Additionally, the FBR's rules on IPR enforcement, which have gone through multiple rounds of revision and stakeholder comment, including most recently in 2015, are being finalized. Even prior to the enactment of FBR rules, Pakistan launched an e recordation system for trademarks and copyrights in May 2015, complemented by the signing of an MOU between the FBR and IPO Pakistan, to increase the efficiency and effectiveness of Pakistan's IPR enforcement at the border. FBR intends to release the public interface of the e recordation system and implement the FBR's IP Enforcement Rules in the coming months. To address Pakistan's reportedly high levels of unlicensed software use, Pakistan has committed to enact amendments to its Copyright Law. Pakistan has also committed to continue regular engagement with U.S. Government IPR officials, including in the areas of the judiciary, enforcement, and legislative reforms.

Despite these positive efforts and promising reforms, reports indicate that the rates of counterfeiting and piracy in Pakistan remain significantly high, particularly in the areas of pharmaceuticals, printed materials, optical media, digital content, and software. Pakistan has the opportunity to address many of these concerns through the forthcoming legislative amendments. For instance, Pakistan should take the necessary steps through its copyright law reform to address the piracy challenges of the digital age and through its trademark legislation to meet international standards and to streamline the registration process. The United States welcomes Pakistan's consideration of the United States' recommendation to include in pending enforcement legislation provisions that would provide *ex officio* authority to enforcement officials. Pakistan should also provide deterrent level penalties for criminal IPR infringement. The United States continues to encourage Pakistan to provide an effective system for protecting against unfair commercial use, as well as the unauthorized disclosure, of undisclosed test or other data generated to obtain marketing approval for pharmaceutical products. The OCR will evaluate whether Pakistan meets the timelines it has announced for the IPR reforms described in this report, as well as how well Pakistan addresses long standing IPR concerns through legislative reform, provides effective enforcement against IPR infringement, and ensures that the IPR Tribunals successfully provide efficient and effective results for right holders.

TURKMENISTAN

Turkmenistan remains on the Watch List in 2016. The United States conducted an OCR in 2015 to evaluate the possibility of removing Turkmenistan from the Watch List. The OCR evaluated whether Turkmenistan had addressed existing gaps in its IPR legal framework, including by joining the Berne Convention and issuing a presidential level decree, law, or regulation mandating government use of licensed software. During the review, the United States welcomed Turkmenistan's accession to the Berne Convention in early 2016. However, the United States remains concerned with the protection and enforcement of IPR in Turkmenistan. Although Turkmenistan adopted a Law on Copyright and Allied Rights and amended its Civil Code to enhance IPR protection, Turkmenistan reportedly has yet to provide for effective administrative, civil, or criminal procedures or penalties for enforcement of these rights. The United States encourages Turkmenistan to provide these enforcement procedures, including *ex officio* authority for its customs officials. Further, the United States remains concerned about reports of widespread usage of unlicensed software on government computers. The United States urges the Government of Turkmenistan to issue a presidential level decree, law, or regulation mandating government use of licensed software. The United States also encourages the Government of Turkmenistan to take legislative action to provide adequate copyright protection for foreign sound recordings such as through implementation of the WPPT or the Geneva Phonograms Treaty. The United States stands ready to assist Turkmenistan through enhanced engagement or technical assistance, if requested.

UZBEKISTAN

Uzbekistan remains on the Watch List in 2016. Over the last year, Uzbekistan continued to make little progress toward strengthening its protection of IPR. The United States urges the Uzbek Parliament to take several critical legislative steps to address longstanding deficiencies in IPR protection: (1) approve Uzbekistan joining the Geneva Phonograms Convention; (2) approve Uzbekistan's accession to the WIPO Internet Treaties; and (3) take legislative action to provide adequate copyright protection for foreign sound recordings. Further, Uzbekistan should provide additional resources to the Agency for Intellectual Property and other enforcement agencies in addition to granting *ex officio* authority to customs and criminal law enforcement officials in order to initiate investigations and enforcement actions, including at the border. Uzbekistan also lacks deterrent level penalties for IPR infringement. The United States welcomes the opportunity to engage with Uzbekistan on these matters.

NEAR EAST, INCLUDING NORTH AFRICA

EGYPT

Egypt remains on the Watch List in 2016. The United States notes Egypt's public awareness campaign which emphasized the importance of trademarks in Egypt. However, although Egypt has taken steps to improve IPR enforcement, challenges and concerns remain. Of particular concern is the failure to combat reportedly widespread usage of pirated and counterfeit goods, including software, music, and videos, and the failure to implement a transparent and reliable patent registration system. Egypt should provide customs officials *ex officio* authority to identify and seize counterfeit and pirated goods at the border. An effective system does not exist for notifying interested parties of marketing approvals for generics in a manner that would allow for the early resolution of potential patent disputes. The United States urges Egypt to clarify its protection against the unfair commercial use, as well as unauthorized disclosure, of undisclosed test or other data generated to obtain marketing approval for pharmaceutical products. The United States urges Egypt to establish and empower the specialized body that is responsible for IPR protection under the Egyptian Constitution of 2014. The United States appreciates Egypt's recent engagement on IPR issues with stakeholders and stands ready to work with Egypt to improve its IPR regime.

LEBANON

Lebanon remains on the Watch List in 2016. The United States welcomes the continued efforts of the Ministry of Economy and Trade's Intellectual Property Protection Office and law enforcement agencies to strengthen Lebanon's administrative and enforcement capacity for IPR protection, and urges the commitment of additional resources to support this work. The United States also recognizes that law enforcement agencies in Lebanon have worked to prioritize actions against counterfeit products that threaten public health and safety, including counterfeit pharmaceuti cals. The United States encourages Lebanon to make progress on pending IPR legislative reforms, including with respect to draft laws (concerning trademark, GIs, and industrial designs) as well as amendments to Lebanon's copyright and patent laws. The United States also encourages Lebanon to ratify and implement the latest acts of several IPR framework treaties, including the Paris Convention for the Protection of Industrial Property, the Berne Convention, and the Nice Agreement Concerning the International Classification of Goods and Services for the Purposes of the Registration of Marks. In addition, the United States encourages Lebanon to ratify and implement the Singapore Treaty, and join the Patent Cooperation Treaty and the Madrid Protocol. The United States continues to stress the importance of Lebanon providing its Cyber Crime and Intellectual Property Rights Bureau and Customs with *ex officio* enforcement authority and its enforcement authorities with adequate resources to carry out their IPR enforcement functions. The United States looks forward to continuing to work with Lebanon to address these and other issues.

EUROPE AND EURASIA

BULGARIA

Bulgaria remains on the Watch List in 2016. The United States continues to have serious concerns regarding Bulgaria's protection and enforcement of IPR. Internet and cable television piracy in Bulgaria remain particularly troubling. This is due in part to gaps in Bulgaria's law with respect to the exclusive rights granted to copyright and related right holders, including with respect to copyright and enforcement over the Internet. In addition, Bulgaria's enforcement of IPR remains a concern. The United States therefore encourages Bulgaria to make the legal reforms necessary to protect IPR adequately and effectively as well as to enhance its enforcement efforts under existing law, which appear to be diminishing, including with respect to online piracy. For example, the division responsible for online piracy enforcement has been reorganized, and its jurisdiction limited, thereby further reducing efforts to combat copyright infringement over the Internet by websites hosted in Bulgaria or operated by Bulgarians. The United States encourages Bulgaria to enhance the role of this IPR enforcement division and to devote the necessary resources to improving the prosecution of IPR cases. For instance, the United States encourages the Prosecutor General to establish specialized IPR prosecutorial units in Sofia and other large cities, appoint a sufficient number of lawyers to these units, provide detailed guidance and training, and closely monitor and analyze their work. The United States also encourages Bulgaria to take steps to improve the efficiency of its judicial system in dealing with IPR cases, and to impose deterrent penalties for those who are convicted of IPR crimes. The United States looks forward to continuing to work with Bulgaria to address these and other issues.

GREECE

Greece remains on the Watch List in 2016. The United States welcomes the amendments made by Greece to its Code of Civil Procedure (which entered into force on January 1, 2016), and its introduction of draft legislation to address copyright piracy over the Internet (which occurred on December 23, 2015). While the United States welcomes these developments, U.S. concerns continue with respect to several IPR protection and enforcement issues in Greece. Generally, Greece's prioritization of IPR protection and enforcement appears to have diminished. The United States understands, for example, that neither the inter ministerial IPR coordinating committee nor the public private online piracy working groups met in 2015. Specifically, concerns remain with respect to copyright protection, as well as enforcement issues, including regarding border and criminal enforcement. The United States encourages Greece to implement measures to combat public and private use of infringing software. The United States also encourages Greece to bolster its system for combating piracy over the Internet, including by strengthening its legal regime and enhancing enforcement efforts. With respect to customs enforcement, the United States urges Greece to enact official storage time limits for goods detained at Greek ports and to ensure the timely destruction of these goods, as well as to consider joining most EU member states in adopting a policy that allows for the inspection and detention of counterfeit goods in transit. Finally, the United States urges Greece to address persistent problems with criminal enforcement delays and reports of judges' reluctance to impose deterrent sentences and penalties on large scale infringers. The United States looks forward to continuing to work with Greece to address these and other issues.

ROMANIA

Romania remains on the Watch List in 2016. While the United States welcomes working level cooperation in Romania between industry and law enforcement authorities, including prosecutors and police, concerns continue with respect to the lack of priority Romania appears to place on IPR enforcement. The United States encourages Romania to enhance its IPR enforcement activities, including in the following ways. The United States urges Romania to develop a national IPR enforcement strategy through the inter ministerial Intellectual Property Working Group, which would include the appointment of a high level intellectual property enforcement coordinator, responsible for directing the development and implementation of the national strategy. Romania should also fully staff and fund the IPR Coordination Department in the General Prosecutor's Office, and encourage the Department to prioritize its investigation and prosecution of significant IPR cases. Romania should also provide adequate resources (including necessary training), high priority support, and instructions to prioritize IPR cases for all specialized police, customs, and local law enforcement. The United States looks forward to continuing to work with Romania to address these and other issues.

SWITZERLAND

Switzerland is placed on the Watch List in 2016. Generally speaking, Switzerland broadly provides high levels of IPR protection and enforcement in its territory. Switzerland makes important contributions to promoting such protection and enforcement internationally, including in bilateral and multilateral contexts, which are welcomed by the United States. However, the decision to place Switzerland on the Watch List this year is premised on U.S. concerns regarding specific difficulties in Switzerland's system of online copyright protection and enforcement. Six years have elapsed since the issuance of a decision by the Swiss Federal Supreme Court, which has been implemented to essentially deprive copyright holders in Switzerland of the means to enforce their rights against online infringers; enforcement is a critical element of providing meaningful IPR protection. Since 2010, right holders report that Switzerland has become an increasingly popular host country for infringing websites, as indicated in the 2015 Notorious Markets List. The United States welcomes the steps taken by Switzerland in response to this serious concern, including the creation of stakeholder roundtables to develop recommendations to address these concerns and the introduction of draft copyright legislation. However, more remains to be done and the United States continues to encourage the Swiss government to move forward expeditiously with concrete and effective measures that address copyright piracy in an appropriate and effective manner, including through legislation, administrative action, consumer awareness, public education, and voluntary stakeholder initiatives. The United States looks forward to cooperating with Switzerland to address these and other intellectual property related challenges.

TURKEY

Turkey remains on the Watch List in 2016 and the United States' concerns continue to rise. Turkey made little to no progress on IPR issues in 2015, and enforcement of existing IPR laws, particularly by the judiciary, remains extremely weak. Given Turkey's prominent role as a source and transshipment point of counterfeit goods, the government must make fundamental improvements in the country's IPR and enforcement regimes, including enhancing Turkey's border control measures. Currently, the Government of Turkey does not have an effective mechanism for ensuring the use of licensed software domestically. The most recent available data indicate that the rate of unlicensed software use by the Government of Turkey is 60 percent, representing a commercial value of $504 million. Stakeholders report that enforcement against unauthorized use of software slightly improved recently, but also noted that the system could be further improved by encouraging judges to issue deterrent sentences and damage awards in criminal and civil cases, respectively. It is unclear whether Turkey will act on many promised IPR legislative reforms that have been discussed for the past several years. Legislation would be appropriate to improve several deficiencies in the system: the copyright law should be amended to provide an effective mechanism to address piracy in the digital environment, including full implementation of the WIPO Internet Treaties; royalty collecting societies should be required to have fair and transparent procedures; and the Turkish National Police (TNP) should be given the *ex officio* authority they currently lack, which impedes police from acting on obvious infringement cases. Turkey should also ease the process for TNP to obtain search and seizure warrants for suspected IP infringement. The United States continues to encourage Turkey to clarify how it protects against the unfair commercial use, as well as unauthorized disclosure, of undisclosed test or other data generated to obtain marketing approval for pharmaceutical products. The United States urges Turkey to be consistent with its own legislation on its regulatory approval timeline (currently 210 days for pharmaceuticals approved by any EU member state) and, in particular, to eliminate regulatory delays that stem from nontransparent procedures or practices. Finally, U.S. industry continues to express significant concerns regarding the lack of efficiency, transparency, and fairness in the pharmaceutical manufacturing inspection process.

WESTERN HEMISPHERE

CANADA

Canada remains on the Watch List in 2016. The United States welcomed Canada's amendment to its Copyright Act to extend protection for sound recordings to 70 years from the date of the recording. However, the United States continues to urge Canada to fully implement its commitments pursuant to the WIPO Internet Treaties and to continue to address the challenges of copyright piracy in the digital age. The United States remains deeply concerned that Canada does not provide customs officials with the ability to detain pirated and counterfeit goods that are moving in transit or are transshipped through Canada. As a result, the United States urges Canada to provide its customs officials with full *ex officio* authority to improve its ability to address the serious problem of pirated and counterfeit goods entering our highly integrated supply chains. With respect to pharmaceuticals, the United States continues to have serious concerns about the availability of rights of appeal in Canada's administrative process for reviewing regulatory approval of pharmaceutical products as well as about the breadth of the Minister of Health's discretion in disclosing confidential business information. The United States also continues to have serious concerns about the lack of clarity and the impact of the heightened utility requirements for patents that have been imposed by Canadian courts. In these cases, courts have invalidated valuable patents held by U.S. pharmaceutical companies on utility grounds, by interpreting the "promise" of the patent and finding that insufficient information was provided in the application to substantiate that promise. These recent decisions, which have affected products that have been in the market and benefiting patients for years, have led to uncertainty for patent holders and applicants, including with respect to how to effectively meet this standard. This unpredictability also undermines incentives for investments in the pharmaceutical sector. The United States understands that the Supreme Court of Canada may have the opportunity to clarify this doctrine in the coming year. The United States urges Canada to engage meaningfully with affected stakeholders and the United States on patent utility issues. The United States also looks forward to working closely with Canada in the coming year to explore ways to address each country's IPR priority issues.

Under the TPP Agreement, which sets strong and balanced standards on IPR protection and enforcement (See Trans Pacific Partnership), Canada has committed to strengthen its IPR regime in many of these, as well as other, areas. The United States will work closely with Canada on TPP implementation.

MEXICO

Mexico remains on the Watch List in 2016. One significant positive development in 2015 was the creation of the Digital IP Crime Unit by the Specialized IP Unit of the Attorney General's Office to investigate and prosecute Internet crimes. The Specialized IP Unit also worked with right holders to conduct several raids against two notorious markets located in Mexico, the Tepito Market and the San Juan de Dios Market. However, serious concerns remain, particularly with respect to the widespread availability of pirated and counterfeit goods in these markets and throughout Mexico, including goods made available by Transnational Criminal Organizations. Infringement cases are extremely lengthy and appeals of initial decisions can continue for over 10 years. To combat these high levels of IPR infringements, Mexico needs to improve coordination among federal and sub federal officials, devote additional resources to enforcement, bring more IPR related prosecutions, and impose deterrent penalties against infringers. The United States continues to urge Mexico to enact legislation to modernize its copyright regime, including by fully implementing the WIPO Internet Treaties and providing more deterrent enforcement against the unauthorized camcording of motion pictures in theaters. Additionally, Mexico's enforcement against suspected infringing goods at the border remains hampered. Prior to 2011, Mexican customs authorities and the Attorney General's Office worked jointly to intercept and prosecute in transit shipments of counterfeit and pirated goods. A subsequent shift in policy, however, has resulted in Mexican authorities only being able to take criminal action against in transit shipments of suspected infringing goods if there is evidence of "intent for commercial gain" in the Mexican territory, which is very difficult to determine. The United States strongly urges Mexico to provide its customs officials with *ex officio* authority and to revert to the previous policy that allowed for the interception of potentially dangerous goods bearing counterfeit trademarks moving in transit to the United States and other countries.

Under the TPP Agreement, which sets strong and balanced standards on IPR protection and enforcement (See Trans Pacific Partnership), Mexico has committed to strengthen its IPR regime in many of these, as well as other, areas. The United States will work closely with Mexico on TPP implementation, including through robust bilateral engagement on issues of mutual concern, and technical assistance.

COSTA RICA

Costa Rica remains on the Watch List in 2016. The United States welcomes the reduction in the monetary threshold for criminal counterfeit trademark prosecutions and the slight increase in the number of ongoing criminal investigations. The United States also applauds the increased intra government coordination on IP. While the Economic Crimes Prosecutor has taken on responsibilities for IP, it remains unclear whether the Government of Costa Rica has committed the necessary resources to effectuate lasting improvements in IP enforcement. To allow more transparency regarding the effectiveness of IPR prosecutions in Costa Rica, the government should publish annually detailed information by type of IP right involved on the number of cases opened, cases resulting in charges, case resolution, and any resulting sentences. The United States also welcomes reports that Costa Rican ministries have recently concluded audits as to their use of unlicensed software but urges Costa Rica to close the unlicensed software gap in the coming year. The United States urges Costa Rica to take effective action against any notorious online markets within its jurisdiction that specialize in unlicensed works and to address the concern that Costa Rican law still allows online service providers 45 days to forward infringement notices to subscribers. Pharmaceutical and agricultural chemical patent holders report various concerns, including as to Costa Rica's data exclusivity regime and extensive delays in regulatory approvals. Further, certain rulings on applications to register GIs present uncertainty regarding market access, as determinations appeared not to take into account evidence vital in determining whether elements of a compound GI are considered generic in Costa Rica. In order to improve border enforcement, Costa Rica should create a formal customs recordal system for trademarks to allow customs officers to make full use of their ex officio authority to detain and examine goods. The

United States urges Costa Rica to build on initial positive steps, to develop clear plans, to continue to tackle longstanding problems, and to demonstrate clear progress in implementing those plans prior to the next Special 301 Report.

DOMINICAN REPUBLIC

The Dominican Republic remains on the Watch List in 2016. Positive developments include a successful enforcement action against a counterfeit medicines manufacturing and distribution network, a modest reduction in the large backlog of pending patent applications, and the launch of an online patent database. Nevertheless, substantial IPR concerns remain, including the widespread availability of pirated and counterfeit products, and government and private sector use of unlicensed software. The unauthorized retransmission of satellite signals is an additional major problem that has been insufficiently addressed by government authorities. Across the board, enforcement efforts are hampered by lack of intellectual property expertise and emphasis from prosecutors and the judiciary. The still large patent application backlog underscores the need for patent term adjustment for unreasonable administrative delays, however, applications for adjustment continue to be denied at the administrative level. Additionally, the United States urges the Government of the Dominican Republic to increase transparency and predictability in protecting undisclosed test or other data generated to obtain marketing approval for pharmaceutical products against unfair commercial use and unauthorized disclosure by issuing regulations governing the process. The United States urges the Dominican Republic to take clear actions in 2016 to improve IPR protection and enforcement.

GUATEMALA

Guatemala remains on the Watch List in 2016. Rulings in Guatemala on applications to register GIs appear sound and well reasoned for compound GI names. However, due to a ruling by administrative authorities on GI protection for single name cheeses, concerns arose regarding new U.S. exporters' ability to export certain types of cheeses and other products to Guatemala. The United States urges the Government of Guatemala to provide greater clarity in the scope of protections for GIs, including by providing clear notice to the public as to generic terms, including any that are elements of a compound GI. The United States continues to engage actively with the Guatemalan Ministry of Economy, the Attorney General's Office, and the Intellectual Property Registry on this important issue. Despite a generally sound IPR legal framework, enforcement activities in Guatemala remain limited due to resource constraints and lack of coordination among law enforcement agencies. Additionally, the United States urges the Government of Guatemala to strengthen enforcement, including criminal prosecution, and administrative and customs border measures. Pirated and counterfeit goods continue to be widely available and Guatemala has reportedly become a source of counterfeit pharmaceutical products sold in country and elsewhere. Trademark squatting is a significant concern, impacting the ability of legitimate businesses to use their marks, as administrative remedies are inadequate and relief through the courts is slow and expensive. Cable signal piracy and government use of unlicensed software are also serious problems that remain largely unaddressed. The United States urges Guatemala to take clear and effective actions in 2016 to improve the protection and enforcement of IPR in Guatemala in 2016.

BARBADOS

Barbados remains on the Watch List in 2016. While the legal framework in Barbados largely addresses IPR, the United States continues to have concerns about the interception and retransmission of U.S. cable programming by local cable operators in Barbados and throughout the Caribbean region without the consent of, and without adequately compensating, U.S. right holders. The United States also has continuing concerns about the refusal of Barbadian TV and radio broadcasters and cable and satellite operators to pay for public performances of music. (See CARICOM). The United States urges the Government of Barbados to take all administrative actions necessary, without undue delay, to ensure that all composers and songwriters receive the royalties they are owed for the public performance of their musical works. In one case, the local performance rights organization (PRO) won a case before the Supreme Court regarding the appropriate tariff to be paid for broadcasts of its members' music in 2007, and over eight years after that decision the PRO still has not received its monies. While the Copyright Tribunal set a rate in June 2015, that ruling remains unenforceable until such time as it is issued in writing. Moreover, the ruling reportedly recommended a waiver of tariffs owed over the past decade. In addition, the United States urges the Government of Barbados to adopt modern copyright legislation that protects works in both physical and online environments and to take steps to prevent the unauthorized and uncompensated retransmission of copyrighted musical and audiovisual content. The United States looks forward to working with Barbados to resolve these issues.

JAMAICA

Jamaica remains on the Watch List in 2016. In the area of copyright protection, Jamaica made significant progress in June 2015 with the passage of amendments to the Copyright Act to fulfill its obligations under the WIPO Internet Treaties and to extend the term of copyright protection. Jamaica is one of several Caribbean countries with deficiencies related to the unlicensed and uncompensated cablecasting and broadcasting of copyrighted music. (See CARICOM). Jamaica maintains a statutory licensing regime for the retransmission of copyrighted television programming but has not consistently enforced the payment of statutory royalties to right holders. Jamaica has, however, taken some promising steps to ensure that its regulatory agencies are monitoring broadcasting entities. In April 2015, the Broadcasting Commission of Jamaica publically identified 98 channels as being illegally transmitted and issued a directive to cable licensees to cease the illegal transmission of 19 channels by August 2015. This first phase of enforcement action has been met with widespread compliance. However, subsequent removals have not been mandated and dozens of additional channels continue to be broadcast illegally by local operators. The United States also continues to encourage Jamaica to adopt the long awaited Patent and Designs Act, which has been under review for over a decade. The United States looks forward to working with Jamaica to address these issues.

BOLIVIA

Bolivia remains on the Watch List in 2016. While Bolivia's legal framework addresses IPR, the lack of adequate enforcement has been a consistent problem. Stakeholders report that prosecutors rarely file criminal charges, civil suits face long delays, and customs authorities lack personnel and budgetary resources. Video, music, and software piracy rates are among the highest in Latin America, and rampant counterfeiting persists. The United States is concerned by reports that Bolivia, in particular its free zone ports, is becoming an increasingly popular route for the distribution of counterfeit goods in the region. While there have been some successful seizures by Bolivian authorities leading to destruction of counterfeit goods, obtaining assistance from Bolivian customs and the National Intellectual Property Service remains challenging. The United States encourages Bolivia to take the necessary steps to improve its poor enforcement of IPR, including by continuing to expand its public awareness efforts, increasing training of government technical experts, cooperating with right holders on enforcement, and improving coordination among Bolivian enforcement authorities and with the authorities of its neighboring countries.

BRAZIL

Brazil remains on the Watch List in 2016. In 2014 and 2015, Brazil carried out important enforcement actions and brought cases against operators of online piracy sites. Significant concerns remain with respect to the high levels of counterfeiting and piracy in Brazil, including Internet piracy. Increased emphasis on enforcement at the tri border region, as well as stronger deterrent penalties, are needed to make sustained progress on these IPR concerns. The National Council on Combating Piracy and Intellectual Property Crimes (CNCP) was identified in past years as an effective entity for carrying out public awareness and enforcement campaigns, but the CNCP was underutilized and did not deliver similar accomplishments in 2015. In the run up to the 2016 Summer Olympics, the United States urges Brazil to strengthen its commitment and provide adequate resources to IP enforcement. The United States also remains concerned that long delays in the examination of patents and trademarks persist with a reported pendency average of three years for trademarks and 11 years for patents. Brazil took a step to address the patent backlog in early 2016 when agreement was reached on a United States Brazil Patent Prosecution Highway pilot program to expedite the patent examination process in Brazil for inventions related to the oil and gas sector. However, the National Sanitary Regulatory Agency's (ANVISA) duplicative review of pharmaceutical patent applications still lacks transparency, exacerbates delays of patent registrations for innovative medicines, and has prevented patent examination by the National Institute of Intellectual Property (INPI). While Brazilian law and regulations provide for protection against unfair commercial use of undisclosed test and other data generated to obtain marketing approval for veterinary and agricultural chemical products, similar protection is not provided for pharmaceutical products. The United States remains concerned about actions taken by INPI to invalidate or shorten the term of certain "mailbox" patents for pharmaceutical and agricultural chemical products. Strong IPR protection, available to both domestic and foreign right holders alike, provides a critical incentive for businesses to invest in future innovation in Brazil. The United States looks forward to engaging constructively with Brazil to build a strong IPR environment and to address remaining concerns.

COLOMBIA

Colombia remains on the Watch List in 2016. In 2015, the Government of Colombia took steps toward completing implementation of certain provisions of the United States Colombia Trade Promotion Agreement (CTPA), including drafting copyright law amendments and clarifying Colombia's instrument of accession to the Budapest Treaty. However, the copyright amendments must still be introduced and passed, and Colombia's ratification of the Budapest Treaty is not yet complete. Other improvements are still needed with respect to implementation of significant IPR related commitments made under the CTPA, including commitments to address the challenges of copyright piracy in the digital age and accession to UPOV 91. As online piracy, particularly via mobile devices, continues to grow, Colombian law enforcement authorities with relevant jurisdiction, including the National Police and the Attorney General, have yet to conduct meaningful and sustained investigations and prosecutions against the operators of significant large pirate websites and mobile applications based in Colombia. The government has also not been able to reduce significantly the large number of pirated and counterfeit hard goods crossing the border or being sold at Bogota's San Andresitos markets, on the street, and at other distribution hubs around the country. Besides tackling online and mobile piracy, the United States urges Colombia to focus enforcement efforts on disrupting organized trafficking in illicit goods, including in the border and free trade zone areas. The National Development Plan (NDP) 2014 2018 became law in June 2015 and contains provisions that could improve the IPR environment in Colombia, such as a requirement to develop an IPR enforcement policy to help guide, coordinate, and raise awareness of IPR enforcement. However, other NDP provisions, depending on how they are interpreted and implemented, may undermine innovation and IP systems (e.g., establishing a role for the health ministry in the examination of pharmaceutical patent applications). USTR will conduct an OCR in 2016 to evaluate, at appropriate intervals, Colombia's commitment to the CTPA and to monitor its implementation of the NDP. The United States looks forward to continuing constructive engagement with Colombia on these and other matters.

ECUADOR

Ecuador is moved from the Priority Watch List to the Watch List in 2016. While enforcement of IPR against widespread counterfeiting and piracy remains weak (including in marketplaces such as La Bahia Market in Guayaquil), amendments made to the penal code amendments in 2015 that reinstated some criminal procedures and penalties for commercial scale counterfeiting and piracy, as well as Ecuador's willingness to engage with the United States are positive steps. Concerns remain including with respect to Ecuador's draft Code of the Social Economy of Knowledge, Creativity, and Innovation. Ecuador is strongly encouraged to conduct an open, transparent, and inclusive process before advancing this draft law that, in its current form, would represent a departure from international practice and could threaten foreign investment in and further development of Ecuador's innovative and creative industries. Ecuador is also encouraged to bring its patent maintenance fees back into alignment with international practice. With respect to the pharmaceutical and agricultural chemical industries, Ecuador does not appear to adequately protect against the unfair commercial use, or the unauthorized disclosure, of undisclosed test or other data generated to obtain marketing approval for pharmaceutical and agricultural chemical products. Ecuador must also ensure that its implementation of Decree 522 regarding the use of registered trademarks on off patent medications and generic medicines does not prejudice the legitimate interests of affected trademark holders. Finally, the United States encourages Ecuador to provide clarification on its processes related to the compulsory licensing of pharmaceuticals.

PERU

Peru remains on the Watch List in 2016. While Peru continues to make some progress to promote IPR and raise public awareness, including on counterfeit medicines, the United States remains concerned about the widespread availability of counterfeit and pirated products in Peru. Right holders report that Peru is a major source of unauthorized "camcorded" copies and administrators of notorious Spanish language websites are based in Peru. The United States continues to urge Peru to devote additional resources for IPR enforcement, improve coordination among enforcement agencies, enhance its border controls, and build the technical IPR related capacity of its law enforcement officials, prosecutors, and judges. The United States also encourages Peru to pursue prosecutions under the law that criminalizes the sale of counterfeit medicines. In addition, the United States urges Peru to ensure that it implements its existing obligations under the United States Peru Trade Promotion Agreement (PTPA) such as to provide statutory damages; to protect against the unfair commercial use, as well as unauthorized disclosure, of undisclosed test or other data generated to obtain marketing approval for agricultural chemical products; and to establish limitations on liability for ISPs under the circumstances outlined in the PTPA. Peru also needs to clarify its protections for biotechnologically derived pharmaceutical products.

Under the TPP Agreement, which sets strong and balanced standards on IPR protection and enforcement (See Trans Pacific Partnership), Peru has committed to strengthen its IPR regime in these and other areas. The United States will work closely with Peru on TPP implementation, including through technical assistance and other trade capacity building. The United States will also continue to address IPR issues through bilateral engagement.

ANNEX 1
Special 301 Statutory Basis

Pursuant to Section 182 of the Trade Act of 1974, as amended by the Omnibus Trade and Competitiveness Act of 1988, the Uruguay Round Agreements Act of 1994, and the Trade Facilitation and Trade Enforcement Act of 2015 (19 U.S.C. § 2242), USTR is required to identify "those foreign countries that deny adequate and effective protection of intellectual property rights (IPR), or deny fair and equitable market access to United States persons that rely upon intellectual property protection."

The USTR shall only designate countries that have the most onerous or egregious acts, policies, or practices and whose acts, policies, or practices have the greatest adverse impact (actual or potential) on the relevant U.S. products as Priority Foreign Countries. Priority Foreign Countries are potentially subject to an investigation under the Section 301 provisions of the Trade Act of 1974. USTR may not designate a country as a Priority Foreign Country if it is entering into good faith negotiations or making significant progress in bilateral or multilateral negotiations to provide adequate and effective protection of IPR. USTR is required to decide whether to identify countries within 30 days after issuance of the annual National Trade Estimate Report. In addition, USTR may identify a trading partner as a Priority Foreign Country or re designate the trading partner whenever the available facts indicate that such action is appropriate.

To aid in the administration of the statute, USTR created a Priority Watch List and Watch List under the Special 301 provisions. Placement of a trading partner on the Priority Watch List or Watch List indicates that particular problems exist in that country with respect to IPR protection, enforcement, or market access for persons relying on IPR. Countries placed on the Priority Watch List are the focus of increased bilateral attention concerning the specific problem areas.

On February 24, 2016, the Trade Facilitation and Trade Enforcement Act of 2015 became law, creating four requirements with respect to the Special 301 process. First, USTR must assess a country's protection and enforcement of trade secrets when considering the country's listing in the Special 301 report. Second, "action plans" are required for each foreign country that USTR has identified for placement on the Priority Watch List and that has remained on that list for at least one year. Third, USTR must provide to the Senate Finance Committee and to the House Ways and Means Committee a description of the action plans developed for Priority Watch List Countries and any actions taken by foreign countries under such plans. Lastly, for those Priority Watch List countries for which an action plan has been developed, the President may take appropriate action if the country has not substantially complied with the benchmarks set forth in the action plan.

Section 306 of the Trade Act of 1974 requires USTR to monitor a trading partner's compliance with measures that are the basis for resolving an investigation under Section 301. USTR may apply sanctions if a country fails to satisfactorily implement such measures.

The Trade Policy Staff Committee, in particular the Special 301 Subcommittee, in advising the USTR on the implementation of Special 301, obtains information from and holds consultations with the private sector, civil society and academia, U.S. embassies, foreign governments, and the U.S. Congress, among other sources.

ANNEX 2
United States Government-Sponsored Technical Assistance and Capacity Building

In addition to identifying concerns, this Report also highlights opportunities for the U.S. Government to work closely with trading partners to address those concerns. The U.S. Government collaborates with various trading partners on IPR-related training and capacity building around the world. Domestically and abroad, bilaterally, and in regional groupings, the U.S. Government remains engaged in building stronger, more streamlined, and more effective systems for the protection and enforcement of IPR.

Although many trading partners have enacted IPR legislation, a lack of criminal prosecutions and deterrent sentencing has reduced the effectiveness of IPR enforcement in many regions. These problems result from several factors, including a lack of knowledge of IPR law on the part of judges and enforcement officials, and insufficient enforcement resources. The United States welcomes steps by a number of trading partners to educate their judiciary and enforcement officials on IPR matters. The United States continues to work collaboratively with trading partners to address these issues.

The U.S. Patent and Trademark Office (USPTO), through the Global Intellectual Property Academy (GIPA) and the Office of Policy and International Affairs offers programs in the United States and around the world to provide education, training, and capacity building on IPR protection, commercialization, and enforcement. These programs are offered to patent, trademark, and copyright officials; judges and prosecutors; police and customs officials; foreign policy makers; and U.S. right holders.

Other U.S. Government agencies bring foreign government and private sector representatives to the United States on study tours to meet with IPR professionals and to visit the institutions and businesses responsible for developing, protecting, and promoting IPR in the United States. One such program is the Department of State's International Visitors Leadership Program, which brings groups from around the world to cities across the United States to learn more about IPR and related trade and business issues.

Internationally, the U.S. Government is also active in partnering to provide training, technical assistance, capacity building, exchange of best practices, and other collaborative activities to improve IPR protection and enforcement. The following are examples of these programs.

- In 2015, GIPA provided training to 4,024 foreign IPR officials and college students and faculty in IPR related programs of study from 125 countries through 95 separate programs. Attendees included IPR policy makers, judges, prosecutors, customs officers, examiners, and college students, as well as faculty in programs of study and training topics that covered the entire spectrum of IPR.

- GIPA has produced 31 free distance learning modules available to the public. These modules cover six different areas of intellectual property law and are available in five different languages (English, Spanish, French, Arabic, and Russian); and several more topics will be introduced in the areas of copyrights and trade secrets. Since 2010 the modules have been visited over 51,700 times at WWW.USPTO.GOV.

- In addition, the USPTO's Office of Policy and International Affairs provides capacity building in countries around the world and has formed partnerships with 20 national, regional, and international IPR organizations, such as the United Kingdom Intellectual Property Office, Japan Patent Office, European Patent Office, German Patent and Trademark Office, Government Agencies of the People's Republic of China, Mexican Institute of Industrial Property, the Korean Intellectual Property Office, and WIPO. These partnerships help establish a framework for joint development of informational, educational intellectual property content, technical cooperation, and classification activities.

- The Department of Commerce's International Trade Administration (ITA) collaborates with the private sector to develop programs to heighten the awareness of the dangers of counterfeit products and of the economic value of IPR to national economies. Additionally, ITA develops and shares small business tools to help domestic and foreign businesses understand IPR and initiate protective strategies. U.S. companies can also find specific intellectual property information on the STOPfakes.gov website, including valuable resources on how to protect patents, copyrights, trademarks and trade secrets. Additionally, U.S. companies can find webinars focusing on best practices to protect and enforce IPR in China. ITA, working closely with other U.S. Government agencies and foreign partners, developed and made available IPR training materials in English, Spanish, and French. Under the auspices of the Transatlantic IPR Working Group, ITA worked closely with the EU's Directorate General for Internal Market, Industry, Entrepreneurship and SMEs (DG GROW) to establish a Transatlantic IPR Portal that makes the resources of our respective governments quickly and easily accessible to the public. All of the ITA developed resources, including the Transatlantic IPR Portal, as well as information and links to the other programs identified in this Annex, are accessible via WWW.STOPFAKES.GOV.

- In Fiscal Year 2015, U.S. Immigration and Customs Enforcement (ICE) Homeland Security Investigations (HSI), through the National IPR Coordination Center (IPR Center), and in conjunction with INTERPOL, conducted law enforcement training programs in United Arab Emirates, Dominican Republic, Saudi Arabia, Costa Rica, Mexico, South Korea, Kuwait, and Panama. ICE/HSI trained officials and police officers from Saudi Arabia, United Arab Emirates, Qatar, Bahrain, Dominican Republic, Costa Rica, Morocco, Belize, Colombia, Curacao, Guatemala, Jamaica, Nicaragua, St. Kitts and Nevis, Venezuela, Mexico, Panama, and Brazil. The IPR Center also conducted an advanced training program at the International Law Enforcement Academies (ILEA) in Budapest, Hungary for participants from Albania, Romania, Moldova and Hungary.

- In Fiscal Year 2015, U.S. Customs and Border Protection (CBP) provided IPR training sessions to foreign customs officials in Argentina, Brazil, Mexico, Kuwait, the United Kingdom, United Arab Emirates, France, and the Netherlands. In addition, CBP supported an ILEA training in Hungary by providing instructors for an IPR focused training session.

- The Department of State provides training funds each year to U.S. Government agencies that provide IPR enforcement training and technical assistance to foreign governments. The agencies that provide such training include the U.S. Department of Justice (DOJ), USPTO,

CBP, and ICE. The U.S. Government works collaboratively on many of these training programs with the private sector and with various international entities such as WIPO and INTERPOL.

- IPR protection is a main focus of the government to government technical assistance provided by the Commerce Department's Commercial Law Development Program (CLDP). CLDP programs address enforcement and adjudication of disputes, as well as IPR protection and its impact on the economy, IPR curricula in law schools, and public awareness campaigns. CLDP supports capacity building in innovation and technology licensing as well as in patent examination and copyright management in many countries worldwide. CLDP also works with the judiciary in various trading partners to improve the skills to effectively adjudicate IPR cases, and conducts interagency coordination programs to highlight the value of a whole of government approach to IPR protection and enforcement.

- Every year, the Department of Justice with funding from and in cooperation with the Department of State and other U.S. agencies provides technical assistance and training on IPR enforcement issues to thousands of foreign officials around the globe. Topics covered in these programs include investigating and prosecuting IPR cases under various criminal law and criminal procedure statutes; disrupting and dismantling organized crime networks involved in trafficking in pirated and counterfeit goods; fighting infringing goods that represent a threat to health and safety; combating Internet piracy; improving officials' capacity to detain, seize, and destroy illegal items at the border and elsewhere; increasing intra governmental and international cooperation and information sharing; working with right holders on IPR enforcement; and obtaining and using electronic evidence. Major ongoing initiatives include programs in Central and Eastern Europe, Asia, the Americas, and Africa.

- The U.S. Copyright Office, often in conjunction with various international visitor programs, hosts international visitors, including foreign government officials, to discuss and exchange information on the U.S. copyright system, including law, policy and the registration and recordation functions, as well as various international copyright issues. Staff participates in a limited number of conferences in the United States and abroad to discuss current copyright issues and inform the public about the activities of the Copyright Office. The Copyright Office also conducts the bi annual International Copyright Institute (ICI) in conjunction with WIPO, providing weeklong training to foreign copyright officials. The 2014 program hosted officials from 15 countries. The next ICI program will be held in June 2016.

The United States reports to the WTO on its IPR capacity building efforts, including most recently in October 2015. (See *Technical Cooperation Activities: Information from Members United States of America*, IP/C/W/610/Add.5)

www.ingramcontent.com/pod-product-compliance
Lightning Source LLC
Chambersburg PA
CBHW080724190526
45169CB00006B/2509